Prayers for All Occasions

BRINGING IN THE LIGHT SERIES

Book I

Prayers for All Occasions

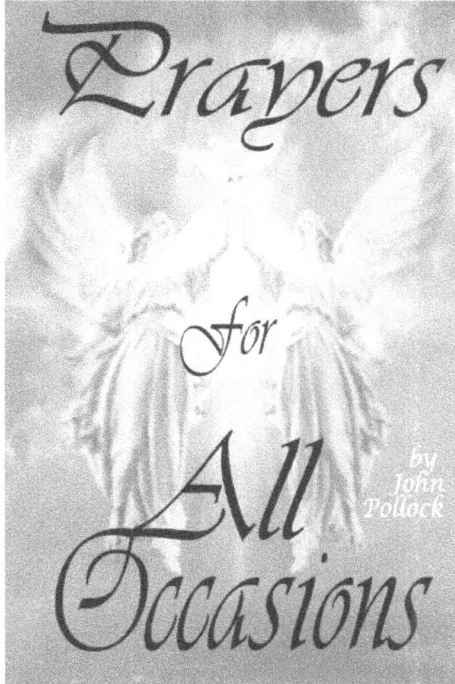

Copyright © 2017 by the Author,
John Pollock

Prayers for all Occasions is self-published by the author.

Prayers for All Occasions

FIRST EDITION

BRINGING IN THE LIGHT SERIES
Book I

Copyright © 2017 John Pollock

The book author retains sole copyright to his
contributions to this book and series

Prayers for all Occasions is written and self-published by the author, John Pollock. All Prayers, Affirmations, and Invocations are channeled by the author unless otherwise notated.

Edited by Jennifer Sweete with author

Cover Art & Design © Laura VanTine, permission to use

Illustrated by John Pollock
Chakra Diagrams by John Pollock
Tree of Life Diagrams by John Pollock and Jennifer Sweete
Medicine Wheel Diagram by John Pollock and Jennifer Sweete
Channeled Light Photo Design by Carol Skylark
Clipart from Public Domain
All Other Acknowledgments within Chapters

Hard Cover
13 ISBN: 978-0-9984448-1-9
10 ISBN: 0-9984448-1-2

Soft Cover
13 ISBN: 978-0-9984448-0-2
10 ISBN: 0-9984448-0-4

Greater is the God within
than anything that dwells without.

- John Pollock

Dedication

This book is dedicated to Love and Light, and the workings of Spirit on many levels. The many blessings on my path have continued to open my heart and eyes to new expressions and new possibilities of Love.

I also wish to dedicate this to the following special Light workers who made significant contributions to my journey before passing on to the other side. I pray for blessings and continued guidance for them: Bill John, Fran Seese Marais, Clarice Markel, Dawn De Herrera, Lois Grant, Karen Weiss, Lorraine Rutherham, Star Evans, George Eenhaus Jr., Hanna Kroger, Marcee Baca, and Megan Grey Wolf, among others. We miss their physical company but their Light and heartfelt presence is still with us. They remain beacons of Light shining brightly!

I pray that this book may be the exact right vehicle for Spirit to reach those who are searching for truth. May this writing attract the people who are divinely guided for the inspiration and prayers within.

In Love and Light,
John

Table of Contents

Preface

I am an Angelic Healer and a channel for the Light! I received a tremendous healing experience in July of 1987 that changed the course of my life. I had a vision of Christ above me, brilliant "White Light" coming through my head and trickling down through my body with gold sparkles filling the room and moving around in a clockwise direction.

Since then I have been on a magical journey to bridge higher realms of Light to those who want healing and greater understanding. Spirit brings new insight and potential as well as transformative healing for those who are ready to accept.

Reflecting on thirty-three years of healing work, it's as if my past in this life was a different lifetime in and of itself. It is still a part of my being but the major focus of my life has taken a new direction with new purpose.

Previously, I was married to a loving wife with whom I had two wonderful children. I moved through careers as a real estate broker and stockbroker, always building and moving to different houses to support the growth of our family. My wife and I discovered our paths heading in different directions. We separated in 1980 when our children were still young approaching their teenage years. Both kids have grown and married with lives of their own, ever changing and evolving.

What stands out the most is that my life has been orchestrated with Spirit to enable me to grow, never to control my direction but always to support my expansion of awareness and service to the Light. Everything that has happened has turned out to be a foundation for greater service and even more love in my expression in times to come. The healing insights have always combined to give me increased gifts and increased abilities for healing and teaching.

This brings me to the purpose of this book. Over the course of the past thirty-three years, I have been exposed to individual healing and learning situations that have been the catalysts for my service and my personal growth. I have been blessed to receive inspiration all along the way. Many situations and experiences in my life have inspired me to write different prayers to help others, as well as myself, to shift awareness and bring our energy fields to higher levels.

This book embodies a collection of prayers, invocations, and affirmations that have assisted me on my spiritual path. In addition, I have included an introduction to various cultural and religious traditions that have contributed to my growth in consciousness. I make no claim as to scholarly representation but have tried to present these with respect for the significant insights they have contributed to me. I have found a thread of truth that resonates with me and I am grateful for this opportunity to share this with others. It is my passion and my prayer that these may be useful to you and everyone you know and love.

Amen, Amen, and Amen

Acknowledgments

I've always felt that I had some great mission to complete in my life. I think a lot of us have that feeling. Yet I never knew what my particular mission was. When I received a great healing for myself, I began to feel the purpose and a new direction starting to emerge.

I want to thank my friends in Spirit for always being there for me. Since my personal healing experience, the Archangels and Sacred energies have been with me, leading the way. It's been a spectacular adventure! So full of wonder and surprise, and always a mystery where it was going to take me next.

I want to thank my family—my daughters, Kristi and Kelly, who have loved and supported me through thick and thin, and my loving sister, Kay, who has lent her steadfast support to me in all my endeavors.

Special thanks go to all the teachers and clients that have been a part of my path of service helping me to learn and grow. Projects such as this have always built up momentum, encouraging me to utilize my past experiences to carry insight forward into the next project taking place through Love and Light!

I especially want to thank my loving friend Athene Raefiel who has been my partner in Light and High adventure. She has collaborated on much of the material here. I also wish to thank Judy Edmondson who is consistently helping with my personal release work and supporting my spiritual growth.

Thank you to Bob and Chris, channels for Andryl Angel, for their guidance to write and teach, as well as sharing their earth clearing process to release baggage. I also want to thank Ann Swenson for her spiritual friendship, support, and contribution of her affirmation for inclusion in this book.

Much gratitude to Laura VanTine for the dynamic graphic arts design she provided for the book cover for *Prayers for All Occasions*. Her enthusiasm helped set this project into motion.

Gratitude in abundance for author and editor, Jennifer Sweete, for picking this project up when it seemed to run amuck, and for helping me follow it through to completion.

I extend my great appreciation to Carol Skylark for the wonderful picture representation of me with my guides. Her artistic vision is truly guided by Divine Spirit!

I also wish to express my heartfelt thanks and a special prayer for everyone else who has contributed to make this book happen and to all those that we may touch in Spirit!

I
HOW TO USE THIS BOOK

The most important thing about using a prayer is our personal connection with God, Spirit, or whatever name you choose to represent this omnipotent power and authority that presides over the energies of this amazing universe. That personal connection with God is the foundation of everything I will be sharing with you through this book. If we don't have that connection yet, another person can make the connection or our guides can make that connection for us. It's important to call ourselves to center and to ground, then ask our personal guides to help make new connections with us—always asking Spirit to show us how it works!

Understanding how prayer works is also important. When we put a request out to the universe, the universe scrambles to fulfill that request, especially when the request is an affirmation that things are already done. This is in right order with the Grace of God, of course!

At the beginning of this book, I give some general information about myself and about Angels. Each chapter contains some background information, as well as prayers and invocations to connect with angelic energies. This information helps to make these energies real for us. These prayers and invocations are listed in the table of contents by title of purpose. The rest of the prayers and articles are divided into three aspects:

1) Prayers, Information, and Insights;

2) Affirmations and Invocations; and

3) Prayers and Ceremonies.

In addition, each prayer has a description for its use.

If we are looking for a specific purpose, we can look in the table of contents or simply flip through the book and stop where a prayer fits our particular situation.

At the end of this book, I talk about karma and our potential in life.

I trust this information to be thought-provoking and inspirational, and I release it through Spirit to reach the people who are ready for it.

Let the Light take you on a great adventure!

- John Pollock

II
ABOUT THE ANGELS

This chapter contains inspirational messages from the Archangels about how to work with them. In addition, it talks about how the Angels relate to the Seven Rays along with the Chakras of the body.

This message tells us to call upon Archangel Michael —that He is here for us to help with personal empowerment as well as empowerment of our service.

Most of us call upon Michael in times of trial and ask for help. *Help me with courage, help me with empowerment to resolve difficult situations, help me with higher understanding.* Speaking aloud, we use this prayer: "I ask Archangel Michael to flow through me and help me meet this challenge!"

Another major use of this type of prayer or invocation is to ask Archangel Michael to operate through us so we may feel what it is like to be empowered through the Light. In this way, we may learn how to feel and think in a higher vibration in order to live our daily lives in empowerment with the Light. We may still call upon Michael in times of crisis should the need arise. This use is all about our own growth.

Message from Archangel Michael
to Angel's Grace

Inspired message in meditation, Sedona, Arizona 1990

I am here for humanity, for each of you, yet not to interfere with free will. If you will ask for assistance, the entire Universe of Love and Christ Light, including myself, will open up to you.

My area of focus is empowerment and the un-yielding power of God. I am here to assist with the personal expression of your own truth and to assist in the expansion of awareness of the love that God has for you and for each of us. As we see the power of love expanding within and operating through our lives, we see also that the world has expanded in love as well!

Blessings to each of you, of Love, peace, and joy!

Archangel Michael

Archangels Working with Us

Do you know what the powers of the Archangels are? Do you know how they can help you? Awareness of how the Archangels can enhance your life could finally remove the blockage to fulfilling your unique life's purpose.

First of all, the Archangels *want* you to call on them for help. Don't worry that you might be over-burdening them; Archangels can help many people simultaneously. They also have "armies" of Angels working to support them and assist you in all ways. You can call on them whenever you need powerful and immediate assistance. They will be there to work with you. No job is too large or too small for the Archangels, but be sure to keep in mind that Angels will not interfere with our free will so we must *ask* for help.

The Archangels can bring us the blessings of the universe and Love Divine. In times when things are not moving in ways we would like, often a choice on our part is necessary—many times the choice is very subtle. The Archangels then bring comfort, higher insight and understanding, as well as empowerment through Love and Light.

To work with the Archangels, we simply open our hearts with the intention of emphasizing their attributes through our personal expression. The Love and Light of God, through our joint expression, will operate through us for everyone's highest possible good.

As we read these words now, let us open our hearts together to experience all that we are capable of experiencing and sharing with others, blessing all creation.

---◆---

Message from the Archangels

Inspired message in meditation, Colorado   2000

We are the Archangels. We are aspects of God, devoted to bringing the blessings of love and light to humanity to assist in the evolution of Man and hold the vibration of special gifts for love, peace, joy, and beauty.

We each have a spectrum of special focus in our service to God. The purpose that we each have is associated with a specific color and attribute. We, as Angels, bring God's Will in the most beneficial manner in every instance possible as an envoy of God's Love and Light.

---◆---

Archangels Bringing Seven Rays

After thirty-three years in healing work, this is my understanding of the Archangels and their function. Visualization of the different colors of the Rays, and understanding the purpose of each Ray, tremendously enhances the effectiveness of our healing work. As our clairvoyant sight opens up, we can begin to see aspects of what healing is taking place, and follow along while it is taking place.

Archangel Michael and **Lady Faith,** whose energies correspond with the throat chakra (we will elaborate regarding the subject of chakras in later chapters), represent the strength and power of God on the Neon Blue Ray. This is not the same power as generally perceived on Earth, but rather the quiet power of the unyielding Love of God. **Lady Faith** is the female Archangel on the Neon Blue Ray. Both **Michael** and **Lady Faith** work with empowerment through Spirit and the expression of truth. They teach us that our ultimate empowerment and protection is to anchor light within and operate on the flow of Love and Light through us.

Archangel Jofiel and **Lady Constance,** whose energies correspond with the crown chakra, bring the attribute of wisdom and assist us in receiving guidance. They are a liaison between God and the individual soul level of humankind. This is the Gold Ray. Through gratitude and trust, we may connect with angelic guidance in meditation and receive inspiration and energetic empowerment for our visions.

Archangel Chamuel and **Lady Charity,** whose energies correspond with the heart chakra, work together on the Pink Ray of unconditional love in order to synthesize the conditional human love with the unconditional love from Spirit. They teach us to love and appreciate ourselves as Beings of Light, opening the doors to love others. This also enables us to receive the gift of discernment, which is "a knowingness" as pertains to timing and appropriate decision-making.

Archangel Gabriel and **Lady Hope,** whose energies correspond with the base chakra, work together on the White Ray of purity. Purity restores the soul and blesses our lives with gratitude and an increasing ability to receive. Archangel Gabriel works with inner communication and communication with the flow of the universe as well.

Archangel Raphael and **Holy Mother Mary,** whose energies correspond with the third-eye chakra, work together on the Emerald Green Ray of healing and truth. The Emerald Green Ray purges that which is not truth. They work with us to invoke healing to clear false belief systems that influence health and emotional balance—and all with a sense of humor. Archangel Raphael is also known as the Messenger, purifying and preparing us to return to God upon our death. This is not a bearer of bad news, but rather good news! They teach us to clear discordant thoughts and feelings, blessing our life force here and beyond.

Archangel Uriel and ***Aurora,*** whose energies correspond with the solar plexus chakra, work together on the Ruby and Gold Ray of service. They assist teachers, accountants, lawyers, and spiritual teachers as well. This combines red life force energy and gold wisdom, putting Spirit into action through guidance. They teach the power of truth and love over fear.

Archangel Tzadkiel and ***Lady Amethyst,*** whose energies correspond with the spleen or "sacral" chakra, work together on the Violet Ray of transformation. This Violet Ray combines the first three rays: Neon Blue power of God, Gold wisdom of God, and Pink unconditional Love. These Rays work together to transform our feelings and thoughts. Together as the Violet Ray, these energies clear discordance, release judgment, and promote new possibilities. This transformation Ray is important for balancing karma. St. Germain teaches us to use affirmations, decrees, and Violet Light to transform heaviness into freedom.

Beings of the Higher Order

The 3 M's: **Michael** is part of three aspects of Spirit, referred to as "The Three M's"—**Michael, Metatron,** and **Melchizedek**.

Archangel Michael is the great representative of the strength and quiet power of God on the Neon Blue Ray. He brings us purification, protection, and empowerment.

Metatron deals with sacred geometry, the structure of molecules and the structure of creation. He assists with the balancing of the Gold Ray, which is the will of God, with the Silver Ray, which is the human will on a spiritual level.

Melchizedek deals with guidance for healing, teaching, and service. His energy supports those whose lives are devoted to being of service to humankind. He is the one we call on to just dissolve and take out things that need to be transformed and healed. **Melchizedek** and **Lord Maitreya** were/are important guides for Christ.

Other Important Light Beings

𝓛ord 𝓜aitreya is the Light Being that deals with love and compassion. He brings us a higher understanding of the meaning of love to provide humankind with more compassion and joy, uplifting group consciousness. His energy is directed at helping human beings achieve a state of "Heaven on Earth." His energy is very gentle and uplifting, and is usually felt high up in the crown chakra.

𝓛ady 𝓡amelia works on the Fuchsia Ray or Passionate Pink Ray. She helps to heal and uplift our hearts so we can move beyond heaviness of past experiences and work together with clarity.

𝓛ady 𝓜ihr brings lightness and higher understanding into all relationships. Invoke her to attract others of like mind and similar path as well as harmony, sharing, and synchronicity.

𝓛ady 𝓘srafel, a feminine aspect of **Archangel Uriel,** works with celestial sounds and music to bring bliss and joy.

Guardian Angels

When the world and its troubles become too much to bear and we just don't know which way to turn, that's the time for us to slow down and realize we are not alone.

We have simply forgotten to trust in our Guardian Angels. They have always been with us. Everything we have ever learned about life and how to live came from our Guardian Angels. When we have lost our bearings, we must trust that they will guide us back onto our path. Our Guardian Angels will lift our burdens and refill our souls with energy. They will be with us when we are alone. They will love us when we need love. They will bring joy back into our lives. We need simply to ask for help and they will show us the way to live again.

This is our common understanding of Guardian Angels, reminding us to reconnect with Spirit when we forget to ask, and helping us through our challenges. The Angels tell us that having Guardian Angels is a way for Spirit to extend the Light to us when we need it most. The Karmic Board selects the guides that can best give us help in a way we can understand. Most people don't realize the amount of support that we humans have in living our lives and evolving in spirit. Our guidance is changed in accordance with the speed of our growth and our new level of understanding.

When we choose
our Higher Self
as the truth of who we are,
Transformation
begins!

- John Pollock

III

CHAKRAS, ARCHANGELS, AND RAYS

ach chakra is an energy vortex that operates in the body and is interconnected with all the others. Each chakra has its own color and purpose. Each of the seven Archangels brings a specific ray and a specific focus to work with that chakra for purification and clarity. The result is to bring us closer to our original uncontaminated state of spiritual perfection and to help us to maintain our balance in life.

The soul energy permeates and surrounds the body and contains the lessons that we have chosen to learn in this lifetime. These lessons are set up through the attraction of similar energies from the universe to challenge us to release the harsh feelings that we are still carrying from various past experiences.

With most people, the focal point of the soul is thought to be located approximately three feet above the head. This eighth chakra, commonly referred to as the "soul chakra" and often appearing as sparkling gold light, continually reinforces us on all levels and programs our life lessons. From a spiritual perspective, the focus may be on the evolution of our soul rather than what our personality thinks is important in our lives. It is truly higher awareness of Spirit and of higher levels of ourselves that we seek.

As we proceed to become more familiar with the Chakras and Rays and their corresponding attributes, please note that the Chohan is the keeper for each particular Ray of Light.

CHAKRAS - DESCRIPTIONS

❖ **THE FIRST CHAKRA** is called the "base chakra" and holds a vortex of energy for the physical body and the etheric cell memory.

❖ **THE SECOND CHAKRA** is called the "sacral chakra" and holds energy for sexual and creative purposes.

❖ **THE THIRD CHAKRA** is located in the solar plexus. It is referred to as the "power center chakra" and holds energy for our rational mind involved in the processes of ordinary thinking and logic.

❖ **THE FOURTH CHAKRA** is called the "heart chakra" and is the pivot between lower and higher chakras dealing with love from the personality in balance with higher unconditional love.

❖ **THE FIFTH CHAKRA** is called the "throat chakra" and holds energy for expression. It supports the causal body dealing with the process of empowerment and manifesting.

❖ **THE SIXTH CHAKRA** is called the "third-eye chakra" and works in conjunction with the crown chakra for "seeing" in the mind's eye, knowing and understanding.

❖ **THE SEVENTH CHAKRA** is called the "crown chakra" and brings in higher information and inspiration from Spirit coming through the soul.

CHAKRAS - ATTRIBUTES

1. BASE CHAKRA

CHAKRA COLOR: Bright Red (this is the life force energy referred to as "kundalini")

ISSUES: Survival and fear of death. Issues of extreme fear show up as dark spots in the base chakra.

CALL TO ACTION: Invoke the assisting Archangels to bring in the White Ray of Purity (4th Ray).

ARCHANGELS: Gabriel and Lady Hope

CHOHAN: Serapis Bay

HEALING OUTCOME: The white purifies the red of the chakra, clearing the issues. Unifying inner communications on a cellular level integrates feelings of safety and security.

2. SACRAL CHAKRA

CHAKRA COLOR: Orange

ISSUES: Power, male/female issues, struggle, control, authority, and money. Issues of extreme power struggles show up as dark ropey threads in the base and sacral chakras.

CALL TO ACTION: Invoke the assisting Archangels to bring in the Violet Ray of transformation (7th Ray).

ARCHANGELS: Tzadkiel and Lady Amethyst

CHOHAN: Saint Germain

HEALING OUTCOME: The violet consumes and transmutes the darkness, brightening the orange of the chakra, hence clearing the issues. Single focus and harmony is the key to empowerment.

3. SOLAR PLEXUS CHAKRA

CHAKRA COLOR: Yellow

ISSUES: Fear, anxiety, anger, resentments; hurt affixed through judgment, i.e., "not fair." Issues show up as murkiness, as in yellow being muddied by a mossy green.

CALL TO ACTION: Invoke the assisting Archangels to bring in the Ruby and Gold Ray of service (6th Ray).

ARCHANGELS: Uriel and Aurora

CHOHAN: Lady Donna Grace and Lady Nada

HEALING OUTCOME: The ruby and gold dissolve the fear and anxiety, replacing them with faith, peace, and confidence of Oneness with Spirit, thus clarifying the yellow of the chakra; clearing the issues by adding spiritual purpose to life. Forgiveness brings about the release. Notice how good we feel!

4. HEART CHAKRA

CHAKRA COLOR: Green

ISSUES: Sadness, hurt, and grief.

CALL TO ACTION: Invoke the assisting Archangels to bring in the Pink Ray of unconditional love (3rd Ray).

ARCHANGELS: Chamuel and Charity

CHOHAN: Confucius and Paul the Venetian

HEALING OUTCOME: The pink softens the inflammation of the heart center and opens the heart to give and receive in balance and harmony. This is the synthesis of conditional and unconditional love. Brings together spiritual aspects with that of personality including mind, emotions, cell memory, and physical body. Discernment is the gift of the Holy Spirit!

5. THROAT CHAKRA

CHAKRA COLOR: Bright Blue

ISSUES: Blockage of expression of personal truth and higher purpose.

CALL TO ACTION: Invoke the assisting Archangels to bring in the Neon Blue Ray for strength (empowerment), protection, and purification (1st Ray).

ARCHANGELS: Michael and Lady Faith

CHOHAN: El Morya

HEALING OUTCOME: The neon blue dredges out the blockage and expands this channel, electrifying the bright blue of this chakra. This revitalizes personal empowerment and translates higher truth into action.

6. THIRD-EYE CHAKRA

CHAKRA COLOR: Indigo

ISSUES: Lack of clarity, self-understanding, and spiritual purpose.

CALL TO ACTION: Invoke the assisting Archangels to bring in the Emerald Green Ray of truth and healing (5th Ray).

ARCHANGELS: Raphael and Holy Mother Mary

CHOHAN: Hilarion

HEALING OUTCOME: The emerald green purges the impurities that cloud our inner vision, thus returning the sparkle of clarity to the indigo color of this chakra. This opens the third-eye chakra to knowingness, seeing, and awareness of higher realms, precognition.

7. CROWN CHAKRA

CHAKRA COLOR: Violet and White moving into Gold

ISSUES: Difficulties surrendering to God; faith and trusting information being received.

CALL TO ACTION: Invoke the assisting Archangels to bring in the Gold Ray of wisdom (2nd Ray).

ARCHANGELS: Jofiel and Lady Constance

CHOHAN: El Lanto

HEALING OUTCOME: The gold perfects the violet and white, infusing us with pure consciousness. It is the liaison to the Soul and Higher Self. It is the chakra of wisdom and receiving guidance through practice, clarity, guidance, and self-direction. It brings in inspiration and higher knowledge.

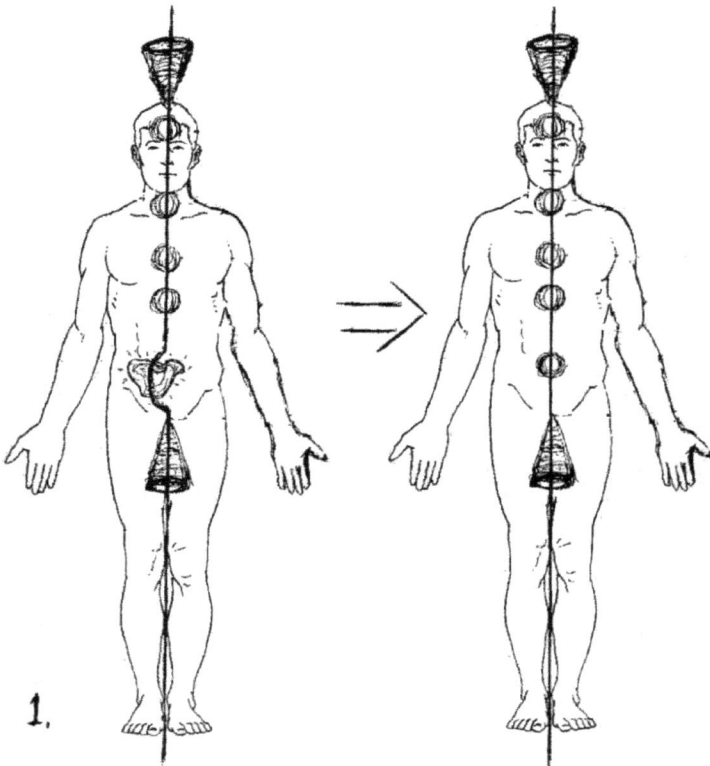

1.

__Diagram 1__ - This is a visual representation of chakras with energy blockage off to the person's right side. The blockage is released and the chakras are brought back into alignment. Alignment of higher levels of consciousness and the energetic chakras gives each level the ability to communicate with the other. This creates what is referred to as a channel where higher knowledge and energetic initiation can come to us from higher dimensions.

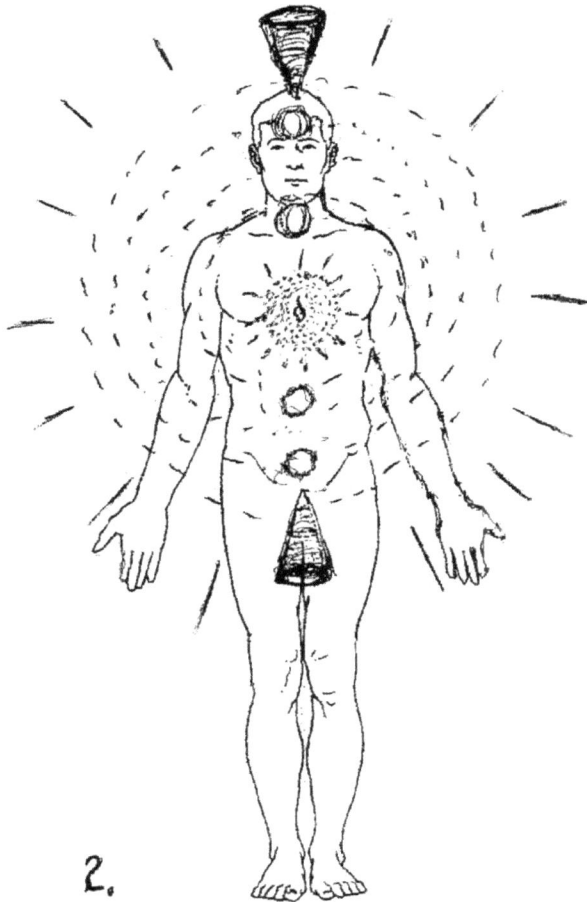

2.

<u>Diagram 2</u> - This diagram shows us another way of looking at alignment with Spirit. It shows Spirit as originating from deeper and deeper levels within our heart. This diagram shows a heart flame and Light radiating out in all directions.

3.

<u>Diagram 3</u> - This diagram shows thinking of energies as alignment of consciousness independent of physical form.

Our consciousness is uplifted on our path to enlightenment. The energies of God also bring energetic initiation, awareness, and empowerment. All life is moved by Spirit. Everything in creation is energy. Light is constantly swirling within creation, helping us to manifest in the physical. It is also swirling back through us, reconnecting us with our most Loving God.

To see energy as coming from deeper levels within our heart means that no outside sources can interfere with our connection with Spirit.

It is important to know that our choice comes first on some level, and then almost simultaneously, our challenges and opportunities are manifested. They appear to us like magic.

The Universe around us tends to behave in accordance with our level of understanding and trust. This knowing is the basis for Spiritual healing and making changes in our life at the core. The energies of God support us and make it all happen!

Knowing that we are a part of God and that God is within us enables us to be empowered in our every intention, truth be known.

Each way of viewing the energies can be beneficial in different situations. The first alignment is good for seeing our relationship with our self, with God above, and with Mother Earth below. We can really feel the descent of Light into our physical world.

Seeing consciousness coming together is helpful at higher levels and between different people. We can use the visualization that works best at the time.

Energies tend to behave according to our understanding. It's a matter of Spirit empowering our free will. What a surprise to discover just how much we can manifest in Spirit. The possibilities are mindboggling.

Beloved Lady Nada tells us it's best to put Christ first, to be in purity of heart, and to be in sincerity. Everything else is up to us.

The Light of God flows down through all levels of creation supporting and sustaining life. The Light also flows through the levels of our energy field for stability and balance in the physical world. We are reminded that we have been granted free will and are empowered by Spirit to create and make changes in the reality that we understand.

Light and manifestation are particularly responsive to our heartfelt prayers. By the grace of God, Christ Holy Spirit, and the perfect order in the Universe, so it is.

Thank you God,
Amen, Amen, and Amen

IV

TEACHINGS, INFORMATION, AND INSIGHTS

This chapter provides teachings and information pertaining to a number of subjects that we all come across at one time or another. It contains articles channeled from Spirit, ending with a formula rub for rubbing on the body to raise vibrations and help with release work.

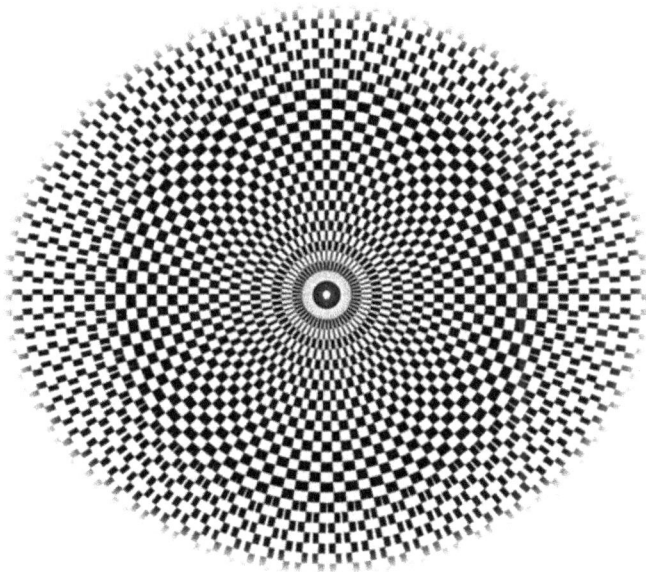

Beginners' Experience
Working with Light

The recommended process for individuals and teachers alike is to follow a set procedure every time that we call all of our chakras into alignment with each other and our inner truth. We call this "centering." We then connect with Mother Earth in a process we call "grounding."

If we are not grounded while we are doing energy work, we will have a tendency to have great experiences but not be able to remember what they are. Therefore, our centering and grounding process is the beginning of all other activity. From here, we connect upwards to higher guidance and ask for help maintaining our center and ground. In addition, we ask to create a sacred space within for channeling, teaching, and carrying out healing activities for others and ourselves.

Experiencing Different Dimensions through the Chakras

We begin by bringing our attention to one chakra. We sense and feel the location and the meaning for that chakra. This experience could be visual in the third eye, similar to a dream experience. It could also be a tingling feeling in the body, or it could be sweetness and/or itching in the crown chakra. It could be ringing in the ears or sometimes even the smell of roses indicating the presence of Mother Mary.

We then move to another chakra. We feel and sense that location—what it feels like and what meaning it has. We can also feel the movement from one chakra to another. This is how we make sense of the symbols of higher and lower energies. The vibration rate moves up as we move to higher chakras, and eventually up to soul level and higher self.

When we visualize and feel from one chakra to another, we begin to notice that they behave as if they are aligning with each other. We then move downwards from our base chakra to connect with Mother Earth and bring Earth energies up through us. We also bring Great Spirit Sky Consciousness into us from above, entering our crown chakra, and then moving through us to connect us with ground and Mother Earth.

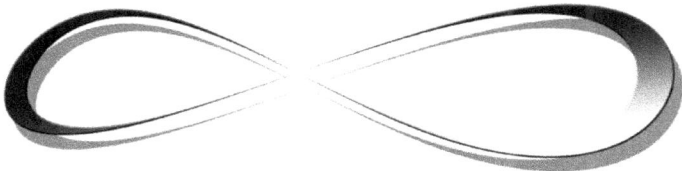

Invoking Spirit and Sacred Space

In a world where we lose ourselves in our own emotions, we often forget our deeper connection to God, and we create our own blockages and dramas. We often wonder where God has gone and why he has forsaken us. When all else fails, we finally return within to our place of peace and point of truth.

From this point, we surrender once again to the Greater God, which then returns us to our proper inner alignment and attunement with Spirit. We remove the patterns we have created that separate us from Spirit, and suddenly God comes back into our lives. The secret of why Spirit appears to us at particular times but not others seems to be directly related to our willingness to surrender to Divine Will.

As a facilitator of spiritual healing, I have been asked to discuss the key factors in assisting individuals to connect with Spirit. Through that connection, we realize the perfection that we already are in Spirit, and we allow that perfection to shine back through to the physical levels, thus allowing healing and transformation to occur.

This process begins with me as facilitator by my surrender to service and highest and best use for the individual in any healing session. I pray for healing Mother Earth as well, and for all with whom we may come in contact. I then work with the process of centering and grounding. There are several different levels of spiritual consciousness that connect us with the Greater God and the rest of the universe.

I call forth in prayer, alignment for the individual I am working with as well as for myself. I call for the personal truth within, our Christ-self, to come forward for each of us. Through that truth, we call to Father and Mother God and to our Spiritual Guidance for assistance to bring us into complete alignment and attunement with Spirit through our soul and higher self.

This invocation actively calls upon Spirit—the God of Love and Light, the Holy Spirit—to help us make connection between God and our personal truth and all dimensions between them.

All Spiritual Consciousness that each individual has access to is the consciousness that may be accessed through Higher Self and that is not subject to Time or Space.

Once connecting with Spirit and aligning all spiritual aspects, it is then important to call our physical, etheric, emotional, and mental aspects into complete alignment with our Christ-self within and our connection with Spirit.

Opening to Channel

The best starting place is through prayer and meditation. Channeling is a spiritual process that sifts through the many aspects and dimensions of our selves to connect with higher dimensions of Spirit.

Imagine a process of moving all of the clutter of our lives to the left and to the right to get it out of the way so we can travel upwards through higher levels of awareness and higher levels of God from whence we have come. This clear pathway moving upwards enables us to bring higher insight and peace and love and understanding, as well as a greater sense of well-being into our lives. This is where the term "channeling" comes from.

Many view this dimensional path as actually being within the heart. They view higher levels of God as actually being deeper and deeper levels in our own hearts. In either case, the image or visualization has a tendency to bring about a higher connection with Spirit and ourselves.

When we sit by ourselves in nature, we experience this process quite naturally and we begin to feel "at one" with all creation and with God. This process allows us to receive inspiration and higher guidance for our lives. When we ask ourselves what we should do in a certain situation and ideas start coming to us, that's exactly what is going on.

As a teacher, healer, reader, or medical intuitive, we show others how to make these deeper connections with God themselves in order to release stress, fear, anxiety, and guilt from their lives. As with anything else, the more we practice, the better we get at it.

There are several things to keep in mind. The most important thing is to first surrender to God for guidance, healing, and miracles. By surrendering, we take ourselves above the level of ego so we can receive Spirit into the physical. In difficult times, if we're asking where God has gone, it is likely that our many personality issues are actually blocking our ability to receive. By surrendering, God magically reappears and we feel supported by Spirit again. Our prayers are answered.

As facilitators, we surrender ourselves to God in service to the Light for the highest and best for all. Without trying to force the outcome, we allow ourselves to maintain a sacred space within us, in unconditional love and with the highest integrity in partnership with the expression and power of God.

We can assist this process by commanding all of our parts to come into alignment with our higher purpose and service. This is called "centering." We can ask our soul and Higher Self to direct this process and bring our personality into alignment with clear purpose and intention. We can ask Spirit to help us to hold a sacred space for clarity and purity of expression. We can ask that we be connected with Mother Earth energy to ground our expression at a practical level. This is called "grounding."

The keys are "Christ first, purity of heart, and service to the Light." From here, we can expand the loving guidance to include highest service possible for others. This may include higher insights and verbal messages for others, or it may include energetic flow of healing, uplifting our "feeling base" to bring a lightness of Being. Gratitude for these gifts makes it all happen and assists us to move into a flow with Spirit. Gratitude makes it all work!

We refer to this as a state of Grace. The ultimate shift is a new awareness of us as an extension of God's essence that is Love and Light.

Making Change

Making change in our life experience involves our recognizing Universal Truth and uplifting ourselves through alignment with God. The universe reflects back to us our view of reality. When we change ourselves on the inside, the things that are happening around us tend to change as well!

The same people around us that we had attributed certain motivations and understandings to begin to act differently; as if all the people we thought we knew are suddenly different people.

By seeing behavior around us from others as a given rather than a mirror of ourselves that is changeable, we miss the opportunity to move ourselves ahead in consciousness. We would miss deeper understandings of others and especially ourselves.

When we have decided to make real change in our lives, it is helpful to view these reflections of other people as guideposts as to what reality we are now creating for ourselves. We can then track backwards from the drama or adventure that we are presently experiencing, to discover the thought patterns that may have created this reality. We are now in a position for growth and transformation.

The more we think that what we see outside ourselves is real the more firmly fixed we become within. As a result we become more resistant to change and growth.

Social sciences, psychology, and philosophy all acknowledge that while we are trying to understand life we are being a key player influencing our observations. In fact, what we *believe* actually creates what we are seeing and experiencing.

That is why we each tend to have a different view of reality. We may have agreement with the group on certain things, but each of us still has our very own personal understanding and life experience.

From our unique base of understanding and experience, each of us formulates core level expectations about how the universe is going to treat us in certain situations. Do we expect relationships to run smoothly or to be rocky with constant surprises? Do we anticipate ultimate success in business or not?

We may be barely aware of these expectations. Yet they act as huge magnets in the universe to attract other people and situations that fulfill these expectations.

If we change these expectations somehow, what we notice is that the same people begin to mirror back to us a myriad of new and different expectations. This will happen or else new people will come into our lives and others will go out in order for the universe to stay balanced.

Letting go of rigid thinking and painful feelings opens the door to new, lighter expectations and more fulfilling realities.

Many of us have experienced great frustration in trying to make these changes in our lives in order to let go of painful drama and create adventure that is more joyous and fulfilling.

On a conscious level, we can choose to expect success and fulfillment in relationships. This begins the process that immediately starts bringing results that are more positive. The universe will automatically structure new situations for us to experience.

As a matter of practicality, these old uncomfortable situations usually bring us closer to Spirit and expand our personal relationship with God. After exhausting all other avenues, we turn back to God for real change in our lives.

In the *Course in Miracles*, Christ says that if we bring unwanted thinking processes to Him that He will gradually bend them around to be in perfect order.

This process of surrendering to Spirit brings about ultimate change and transformation in our lives. Situations where we are unappreciated and unhappy can turn around more quickly than we might imagine.

This brings us to our experience in relationships. Most of us pray to God or look to the universe in some fashion to bring us a partner with the attributes we desire in relationship.

Even though our prayers are heard and answered the "mirror" effect is still in operation. Many times we fail to realize that we have to *be* what it is that we want to *have* in a partner in order to attract a person with those attributes. If we are not the person that we are asking for, then we are likely to attract someone else who is not the person that we are asking for. Likewise, the other person may also be disappointed.

Sometimes we ask for things in prayer and suddenly havoc appears in our lives. At first, we may feel that our prayers are not being answered. However, if we look past appearances we see that God is always there and that it's our own thoughts that confuse or block us from receiving what we asked for.

The principles of prayer continue to operate. Whenever we ask for something in prayer, whatever we have inside that is blocking us will come up to be dealt with.

In addition, we live in a world that is created in love and support through God. From experience, we know that if we change our outlook that it will affect our life. Actually, the truth is more far-reaching than this.

In our first experiments, we may find ourselves in personal, business, or social situations where the drama is bringing about unhappiness, and success is sabotaged. Wanting to have change in our lives eventually brings us to focus on changing ourselves.

This may only come to us after much hard experience. Instead of looking for gain from our every move, we may adopt the simple concept of living our lives as an extension of our truth inside.

When we come from our hearts and give to others without "strings" or expectations, then we find ourselves magically obtaining new friends and receiving appreciation from others.

On a larger scale, God supports that which we choose to create in our lives by giving humanity "free will." Our thinking process and feeling base are the means of communication with God about what choices we have made.

By being down on ourselves, we are telling God and the universe that we do not value ourselves. In this instance, our loving God lends "life support" to our creation. This process may become very painful until we decide we want to appreciate ourselves more.

By honoring ourselves and appreciating ourselves just the way we are, we communicate to our loving God that we are loving ourselves and positive life experiences follow. This is all a grand learning process.

Living in the present moment, maintaining openness to receive, and being aware of our Oneness with God all come together to create change and fulfillment.

By the grace of God, so be it!
Amen, Amen, and Amen

Freedom from Dependency

Issues may arise in friendship, social, or family situations, where we love the people involved but also feel that the interaction is unhealthy or unbalanced with emotional dependency. These situations usually involve issues of victim and rescue.

Guidance has said to detach from whatever drama is going on between yourself and others. Athene Raefiel says we must learn to forgive ourselves, forgive others, and forgive the situation.

We can release the drama just by acknowledging that we are not a victim and that we choose to take responsibility for whatever we're creating. We can then choose to recognize that we are whole and complete. We recognize that the other person(s) also has guidance and is whole and complete.

If we believe someone to be a victim and that we have to help somehow, then we are stuck in the drama. The stage is set to replay the emotional situation repeatedly with no end in sight.

To make a shift, we must make the drama "not real" for them and ourselves, and empower everyone to live from Spirit rather than from circumstance. We focus upon the truth that is beyond the illusion. We release them to be free to create what they want. They release themselves to be free by accepting themselves as co-creators instead of as victims.

We support people to empowerment by acknowledging that they are in charge of their own lives. We are to illuminate but not "fix" the person or situation. In this way, we remind them that they are already empowered in their lives. They are already creating their lives as they are and have what it takes to make change if they want! This brings up the biblical example, "Feed a man a fish and you feed him for a day; teach him to fish and you feed him for a lifetime."

Sai Baba has said that the major challenge for humanity is for us to realize that we are not victims. We are all part of God and a part of God is within each of us. It is for each of us to follow our higher inspiration, allow the flow of Spirit to work through us, and to create new realities.

It is up to us to see through the drama where this applies. It is particularly important to see everyone as whole and as having the same opportunities and the same resources available to us all. We can acknowledge this truth and encourage them to use their resources as well. Likewise, we must see ourselves as empowered!

One of the most challenging things to do is to accept others as having free will and to allow them to live with the consequences of their own actions. We can offer love, emotional support, and encouragement. We support that they can do all the things that they want to do, and do them in a rewarding way if they choose to!

Happy St. Valentine's Day!

This section was written to have fun with St. Valentine's Day and to talk about some of the issues we humans have in relationships. Relationships can be some of the most powerful mirrors of our behavior. We can use them to see our inner selves reflected back to us.

St. Valentine's Day is a celebration for the romantic and the young at heart. It's about the excitement of someone who prompts our heart to sing and heightens our feelings of joy with just the thought of being together. It's about the joy of connecting with that special someone that we feel we may have known forever. Why this elated condition occurs in our lives at certain times and not others has always been a great mystery of life.

Psychologists say that romance is the result of projecting that someone is what we want them to be. We fill in the blanks and assume we have the person of our dreams. The bubble bursts when we discover that the other person is not everything that we had hoped them to be. This can be quite a shock.

The masters tell us that truth is within and that the universe reflects back to us our view of reality. They say it is very useful to view others as an extension of our inner truth and inner process. We tend to draw to us people with similar energies, spiritual focus, and emotional processes. They reflect back to us different aspects of ourselves. Even the thought processes that tend to repeat themselves also tend to be reflected in others and show us what belief systems we are operating with as well.

Fortunately, the universe offers unlimited opportunity for growth and the potential for us to recreate our inner self and our outer reality. In fact, these mirrors become very helpful for us to view these aspects of ourselves that we may be overlooking and be unable to access.

This does not mean that we must spend every waking moment analyzing our lives, but it does mean that by seeing these aspects of ourselves in others we have opportunity to be more of what we want to be. In addition, this means that we can bring what we want into a relationship and allow the mirror effect to show us the best.

Sometimes a mirror can show us the same thing we are doing. For example: *I'm angry with life and now I can see it in another, so I can reflect on how I may be behaving the same way the other person is behaving.*

Sometimes another person may show the effects of what we are doing. For example: *If I lash out at someone, his/her reaction may show me very clearly what the hurt and sadness I'm really feeling looks like.* This is somewhat of a complimentary view of the same situation.

Another interesting thing is the sudden realization that comes when we recognize that a role we are playing with one person is the opposite role from the one we are playing with someone else in our life or perhaps someone in a previous relationship.

What we recognize as mirrors are purely for our own use and not for the purpose of placing blame. Sometimes the views we have rejected in the past appear repeatedly to alert us to important awareness of our own processes.

As these glorious opportunities continually develop, we receive valuable insights and awareness into our own growth and mode of operation. At the same time, we are experiencing moments of warmth and great joy.

It is this joy and sharing on an intimate and personal level that we celebrate on Valentine's Day.

Viva la difference!

Religious Science of "Never" Mind

The purpose here is to remind people not to forget that God is a real and loving consciousness behind the scenes and within all creation. Sometimes when people use a certain format for prayer that works in their lives they may take for granted that the procedure works by itself. They may occasionally lose sight of the nature of the loving God that we have.

Our loving God is the consciousness that encompasses all of humankind, the earth, and all of creation! It is this vast loving consciousness that nurtures and cares for us that we honor as our Father and Mother. This same loving nature cares for us as children and enables our prayers to be answered and to be so effective.

We are God experiencing God from within us. We experience the most expansive, most unlimited, most loving, most progressive, most healing, most fulfilling aspects of ourselves; beyond our experience level, beyond our perception level, beyond our belief system, and beyond our comprehension.

Our intention is to release all that obstructs or interferes with the beauty and love that we embody.

We open our hearts and our souls and ask our most loving Creator to assist us in experiencing our sacred space that lives within by releasing all obstruction and interference that we have created. We recognize our true essence that is experiencing God from within our Being.

God so loves us that God allows us to have the freedom to believe we are in total control. God allows us to modify perfection within the limitations of our mind's thoughts and emotions in order to experience the results. We learn more about the magnificence of God through our expanded perceptions, yet these expanded perceptions of truth still have even more potential for new expansion and new realization. The loving consciousness that enfolds us grows ahead of us and we are a part of it.

Shining Light into Shadows

This is a treatment of the Light with regard to dark-side experience. Focus on the Light is empowerment from the heart. We are not alone in having these scary experiences. The primary challenge is to empower ourselves. We want to be aligned with our inner truth and with Spirit. We want to be at peace and live with purpose and clarity. We want to feel our connection and love from Mother Earth. We see ourselves as one with nature. We go there. We feel the energies of the trees and the animals.

We are gentle with ourselves and take time to meditate and connect with Guidance. When the primary emotion is fear, we dissipate fear and illusion by feeling our fears and letting them flow through us. When we are willing to change, we ask God to help us make it so!

Briefly, we use breath work to breathe in Light and breathe out toxic thoughts and feelings. We take showers to clean our energy field. We do what we must do in order to calm down. We use music, meditation, and incense, and reach out to friends for support. We begin to feel love around us.

Next, we create a Sacred Space, a safe environment to *feel* what it's all about. We identify our feelings. We sit with the fear to get back in touch. We check to see what purpose the fear has served in the past. Can we allow ourselves to feel our unwanted feelings? Eventually, we may come to realize that's all they are—just feelings!

These parts or fragments that we speak of are alienated aspects of our energy field usually containing unresolved issues and feelings that we consciously want to ignore. In addition, the energy field is complex and contains thoughts, feelings, intentions, and higher purpose as well.

When we separate ourselves from our unwanted feelings, we inadvertently push out the energetic parts of our Being that are feeling these unwanted feelings. In effect, we compartmentalize our soul-energy and it becomes one of our fragmented parts. These fragmented parts then begin to act as if they are entities that are separate from us and are being charged with soul-energy coming directly from God. These fragments express their issues and feelings. The rub is that our reality reflects issues of our fragments as well as the rest of our soul.

Through the laws of attraction, our soul naturally strives to trigger our issues and seek resolution. To stop this process from bringing us harsh experiences that seem to come from left field, we reverse the process of denying our feelings. We now feel our feelings, and this tends to integrate the parts of us that we've rejected in the past.

We call ourselves to center in alignment with God and ground with Mother Earth. At the direction of Soul and Higher Self, we call our most important fragments and even our past life experiences to come forward into our vision and into our feeling body. Be prepared to experience intense emotions.

We go back in time to feel the events again just as when they originally happened. This time we allow ourselves to feel our feelings as if they are happening again right now, and we let those feelings flow through us for release. We call our fragments to return home into our heart. We feel our love for those parts of our self and blend them together into oneness. We are one with God once again.

We sit with our fear until it begins to release. Eventually it does. We then find that we don't have to stay in this state of mind. We feel our feelings along the way. The more we acknowledge our feelings and allow them to move through us, the more we strengthen ourselves. We have to feel our emotions before they can be released.

We change our focus. We visualize and imagine seeing ourselves turn around to represent our change in direction. We focus on positive expression, passing any possible interference, while turning the fear over to God. We begin to feel love in our hearts for the blessings of life.

We emphasize feeling satisfaction in our new expression. We become aware that our fear is dissipating, and when the timing is right, we automatically move to a higher plateau.

Say, **"I am the Light Within,"** aloud and as many times as necessary to shift the energy. This assures us that all of the parts that come in really belong to us. We are essentially commanding that all of the parts are of Light. Nothing else can tolerate the Light and they must go! Everything we bring in is a part of us, whether it is an aspect that we like or not. Of this, we can be certain! We feel assured that we are operating in a safe, secure space.

We attract our soul-parts back—not through our mind, but through our heart in conjunction with Spirit. Our mind has been creating this condition all along!

Stop thinking! Meditate with Spirit. We continue to bring Love and Light into our life and into our heart. We feel our love continually build. We sit with ourselves in contemplation. Sit in nature and feel our oneness!

The love inside that we gradually build up is the core of who we are. When it becomes big enough, the love that we carry will transmute the negative thoughts and toxic feelings that we have accumulated. We will gradually gain a sense of our real truth and who we really are.

When feeling trapped in a vicious circle of thinking, then take note. The best way to calm obsessive, compulsive thinking is to live in the present and to minimize the past. Remember that the mind formulates our reality from our perceptions, which are all created by our thinking in the first place.

We must stop using old thinking patterns that give ourselves negative feedback.

Positive interpretations go a long way toward turning ourselves around. What we see is what we get. Our confidence and positive feelings create our new reality, so choose purposefully to look for life-changing positive confirmation.

This is what it takes. Although the overall process is ongoing, we can still make great strides. Our path is totally up to us. We say that changing our life is an "inside job." We don't have to do it all by ourselves. What this means is that the choice or decision must come from within. We then trust that we are supported on the outside by Mother Earth and Father/Mother God! This is our empowerment.

Our mind had invented many dark alleys to travel down in the past. Fueled by fear, it had taken us into desperation and overwhelm. It is now up to us to start following the love and the truth in our heart again. We open our awareness for positive change and we open our love connection with Mother Earth for love and support. Remember, this is a *feeling* process!

Through this process, we can command through our Higher Self and our truth within, that our fragmented parts be returned to us and our missing parts of soul be retrieved. This also applies to child-within fragments that may very well have the same issues as those that the adult is dealing with. God strongly supports our truth and Higher Self.

Since we are on this subject, there is one more thing to know and keep in mind. Many times, people who are seeking to be more spiritual reject their worldly selves while trying to go higher. At some point in time, we all must accept our physical body and personality as part of ourselves again. Integrating our higher aspects back into the body, and healing the split between upper and lower body will be necessary to be whole and complete. We can still be spiritual and be in our bodies. In effect, this is bringing heaven down onto earth.

It is our intention to be whole, and that will act as a strong magnet to attract fragments back to us. We put forth our intention in prayer.

Incidentally, if we are looking for permanent change and it doesn't seem to come, we should closely examine our underlying motivation for attention and/or for excitement. Looking for attention may bring misguided validation. Looking for excitement only attracts off-the-wall drama instead of peace. These unconscious motivations are working against our healing.

Sometimes fear for our survival and fear of not being able to run our own lives will sabotage our ability to take charge of our lives.

The following ceremonial prayer is an adaptation of the Sacred Medicine Wheel. It is designed for centering, alignment, and grounding with Mother Earth as well as integration of our parts and wholeness. It is helpful to perform this ceremony with fire or a candle in the center of our prayer circle, and rocks or additional candles around us to hold energy from the four sacred directions.

The Prayer
Call to Ground and Center
for Empowerment and Wholeness
(to be spoken aloud)

We call our truth to come forward from within our heart, into alignment with our soul, higher self, and God the Highest. We call all aspects of ourselves that resonate with Mother Earth to come forward, and ask her to connect with us in grounding, support, and balance. We feel the surge of energy from deep within Mother Earth coming up through our legs and filling us with peace and contentment.

We honor Mother Earth—the four Sacred Elements of Air from the East, Fire from the South, Water from the West, and Earth from the North—in the names of Archangels Raphael, Michael, Gabriel, and Uriel. We feel the Sacred Energies coming in. We give thanks from our hearts and we welcome you!

We honor Christ Holy Spirit on all levels, the 104 Lakota Sacred Energies, the Hermes levels of existence including God as Source, Aeon, Cosmos, Time, and Genesis on planet Earth, as well as the Hebrew Tree of Life levels for creating and manifesting including Emanation, Creation, Formation, and Action. We feel our alignment and it restores our soul. We honor the Great Spirit and Grandmother, which are the perfect aspects of Mother Earth over time.

We call forth the Mighty forces of Love and Light for clarity and understanding, into union of purpose with the Divas of Nature, the Sacred Elements, our teachers, guides, and God most High, all dedicated to the liberation of our truth and higher purpose.

From higher self, we call all our parts back to us from others. All of our aspects are to be cleansed, returned, and integrated back into us in perfect order. We return all aspects that belong to others. We call for the return of lost soul-parts. We call for all male and female aspects to be returned back and into balance with each other. We release judgments, blame, and issues that no longer serve us. We surrender ourselves to Spirit for higher direction and higher expression of love through us.

We acknowledge and give thanks that we are supported by the Universe and a loving Mother Earth. God, please show us how we are restored to empowerment and wholeness.

Amen, Amen, and Amen

Understanding the Universe and
Our Thinking Processes

I t is good to understand that situations that block positive manifesting are created from the inside feelings of fear, having no trust, and our being blind to support; just as the opposite feelings of confidence and success open us to attract positive manifesting in all our affairs.

While in fear, fear is our thinking and message to the universe. Our fear makes us feel vulnerable. Our feeling vulnerable tells the universe that we have a force that warrants our fear. The universe helps us to make this so, even if we are not aware that the universe is still supporting us. The universe supports the creation of this reality. Our fears are then realized. We receive confirmation in the physical world. We are supported in feeling unsupported! Our illusion is still intact.

When we perceive imminent danger, real or imagined, we move into counter-attack mode. We also inadvertently put our heavy fear and anger into protector status for our defense. Unfortunately, this energy feeds on negative thoughts and feelings, and when there is not enough to feed on it attacks our very self! In this way, we actually create our own demons and we have to transform them ourselves. Often this attack energy has been building for quite some time.

It's familiar like an old friend; yet, we may feel the opposite, that this couldn't be a part of us. It's a matter of discernment. We want to make sure that we're integrating with our own creations.

The tricky part is that we must expand our loving self to be larger than our protector aspect so that we can absorb and transform its energy. It's good to tell the protector that it has done a good job and it is no longer required to do the job.

This is our shift in consciousness. When we now change our position to knowing and feeling that we are safe and supported, and are inherently protected, the universe tends to support that new reality! After all, we have that spark of Light, the Creator within us, empowering our new creation. We receive confirmation of our new reality in the physical world. Our new reality is now supported! We feel confidence and joy.

If we sense the attacking entity is not of our own creation—that is, it is pulling our life force or sending negativity to bring us down—then we bless it and do not accept it. An entity not belonging to us will be attacking everyone else too. We will deal with that situation separately in just a moment.

Fighting against something only gives it power and makes it stronger. The most helpful affirmation is, "I give you no fear, I give you no anger, therefore I give you no power over me! I send you only Love and Light!"

Always looking for attack from dark forces only serves to create, through judgment, an opening in our energy field, and then attracts the enemy to us through expectation.

Feel, see, and know that the primary forces operating in our lives are of Love and Light. Look for signs of confirmation of this truth. First, we see positive possibilities. Later, through faith and alignment with Light we then see our reality shifting.

Choose ahead of time what things we want to experience later that night. Program our nighttime experience. Transform dreamtime. Program our lives!

Honor the Spirit within and choose empowerment. Then, ask Spirit to show us how this is so. Follow guidance! Feel this happening! Feel and know that the primary forces operating in our lives are Love and Light. Again, look for signs of confirmation of this truth. First, we see positive possibilities. Later through faith and alignment with Light, we see our reality shifting.

The purpose of these kinds of experiences seems to be for personal growth and for learning about who we are. It's not about mounting a bigger army, but rather realizing that each of us has a part of God within us, and choosing that as our truth. We release feelings of separation and begin to operate again "as one with God" by choice!

De-possession and Fragmentation

The strongest empowerment and assistance anyone can give to a person dealing with possession and fragmentation is to de-emphasize the significance of what the person is experiencing. Overreacting only heightens the fear levels and feeds the process of disintegration. The person who is experiencing the drama is already in a state of terror.

From a spiritual perspective, we only become fragmented when we accept the drama and our perceptions of illusion as reality. The mind is very powerful! The illusions of the physical and astral worlds can be changed.

To reverse what is happening, we must know and acknowledge that we have a spark of God within us no matter how fragmented we become, even when we think we are no longer present in the body. We can command through our God source that is deep, deep within ourselves, our fragmented parts to return to us through Christ Light and Creator. We must know this beyond all doubt.

Techniques from the Sacred Medicine Wheel align the Four Cardinal Directions and Sacred Earth Elements with our heart and Father Sky to help greatly by energetically clearing and holding a Sacred Space. Sacred Medicine teaches us to align with God from our center and expand Light emanating outwards. This includes our connection with Great Spirit above and Mother Earth below flowing through us. The point is to gradually work our way back and gradually bring in more parts until we can find some peace. Sage and incense are very helpful to raise vibrations in support. We can then feel the love building within us.

Again, we who are re-integrating need to know that if we focus only on the present situation and take positive steps, we can gradually become whole. Things are not as bad as we imagine and we don't have to continue down a scary road. We expand and feel our own love. We turn fear over to God.

We must use our conscious mind to focus on filling ourselves with more Violet Light and becoming stronger in Love every minute! The caution here is to avoid following our fear into negative possibilities. It is the life-affirming possibilities that we want to pursue. Everything new is a creation from our positive thoughts and increased feelings of support from God. We feel the peace and satisfaction from moving in the right direction.

Mother Nature will tend to keep things working in right order on this planet. Normally we tend to see positive possibilities and feel confident much of the time. We look for things to work better next time. Only when we stockpile heavy experiences does the fear build up and work against us.

Prayer for Sacred Space around us and prayer to make us whole again will tend to rebuild our confidence in support and nurturing from Father-Mother God. Seeing it, feeling it, and knowing it will help us to experience it as so!

The person helping stays in a space of love and knowing that the situation is not so bad and that it really can be shifted. We always empower others by knowing that they are strong and have their own guidance. We know that they are coming back together and becoming re-integrated.

If the person working their way back manages to convince the helping therapist that things are much worse than they know, it has a tendency to make things worse. In addition, the client may be sabotaging themselves and even their therapist as well. The therapist must be sure not to buy into the client's drama.

Underlying issues of "neediness for attention" and "fear of non-support" can be handled through child-within processing at a later time. Persons may inadvertently be blocking the healing process by asking for help while subconsciously doing it just to get attention. They may be in fear they are incapable of running their own life. These issues will have to be addressed later, but for now, we want to help the person to gain peace and more balance.

We encourage the person to accept the Love of God that they are blocking. We encourage them to step into their own power rather than running away and abandoning themselves. It is really important for them to accept their physical and their Spiritual power and to ground themselves as one integrated Being. They must release fear of being who they presently are, and release fear that they will be overwhelmed or that their personal power may be misused if they return to the body.

By bringing all these parts together, the person can bring heaven on earth and express him/herself through their one Being in wholeness. They are once again an empowered Being that can go on to teach others how to "get it together."

Energy Attack/Sexual Attack

Despite the similarities, there are some distinct differences here. The underlying issues involved continue to center around empowerment or lack thereof. Fear still helps to create the drama being experienced.

The dynamic has to do with a person being convinced that another person, entity, or situation is stronger. The person is also feeling like a victim and feeling vulnerable. In order to be vulnerable we would have to cooperate with the attacker and live in fear. By feeling fearful and feeling vulnerable we actually give them power against us.

When we're constantly checking to see if another person or entity is crossing our boundaries without our awareness, we have just expressed to the universe our inner doubt about being strong enough or alert enough to keep them out of our space. This automatically opens the door to anyone who wants to take advantage of the situation. It happens on an energetic level. It has to do with control and it has to do with our confidence level with God and our environment.

The same dynamics tend to hold true for women that often get raped or beaten. If this occurs repeatedly, it is because their expectation is that they are vulnerable and that everyone is a potential attacker. This energetic belief of vulnerability attracts what we do not want.

The father of my good friend Clarise once told me a story about his experience on the Indian reservation in South

Dakota. He was visiting with someone from the reservation one day and he asked about voodoo and astral stories within the Indian culture. He wanted to know what was behind the tales he had heard.

The Indian replied, "Nah, there is nothing to it!" There is a lot of wisdom behind his answer. First, he was dispelling the fear and downplaying the drama. Second, even discussing the subject brings up fear in many people, and in this case there was no more discussion.

Judy Edmondson says that the quickest answer for a situation like this is, "I give you no fear therefore I give you no power over me! I send you only Love and Light!" Otherwise, our fear would only tell the universe that we think we are vulnerable to attack.

Minimizing the attempt minimizes the effect. If we laugh at the attempt to scare us, it frustrates the attacker instead.

When someone is experiencing sexual attack in the astral, the most effective thing to do is to release doubt and choose what experiences we would rather have. The desired new experience will block out the old experience.

If we are undecided about what to do, then we are not yet ready for change. It is better to focus on what we want. We want to program our life in the positive. We especially want to program our dreamtime to what we want to happen, including our responses. We should always focus on what we want from higher spiritual perspective.

Another technique regarding energy attack is for a person to visualize him/herself inside a giant bubble filled with gold sparkles of light. Visualize black arrows coming to the bubble, then turning gold and bouncing off.

The same holds true by visualizing ourselves inside a cube of mirrors with all unwanted energy bouncing back to the sender. To stop the game, the unwanted energies can be sent to ground with Mother Earth.

When it comes down to it, the most effective thing to do is to know that we are supported and protected in a Sacred Space with God. This causes us to do what we needed to do in the first place—that is to empower ourselves. We know that we are part of God, and that part of God is within. We are empowered with our relationship with God and being "at one."

"Greater is the God within than anything that dwells without."

Going forth with God empowers our highest aspects of our Self. Any other illusions that have been energized by others can always be dissipated as part of the illusion of the etheric.

Constantly believing that an attack is coming only brings it on. Knowing we are in Sacred Space and "at one with God" inherently carries protection with it. Calling to a loving universe for a place for us to live reduces the anxiety of betrayal by people and our environment. Deception only affects us when we first accept that we are vulnerable to it. We must stay alert and aware of our surroundings while simultaneously trusting our spiritual connection and ourselves.

We must trust ourselves to make the right decisions, and trust Spirit to support us. Turning fear over to God and being confident in a loving universe is an important part of changing our reality and ourselves.

With a passage of time, these kinds of challenges can be seen for what they are. They are situations to test and to teach us about our strength in Spirit. They show us what empowerment is all about.

What counts is our relationship with God, our guidance, and our connection to the Light. It is about our confidence in the face of wild and wooly situations that carries us through. We can choose to live in a universe of love and infinite potential if we want. We can choose to have a life of fulfillment, and realize great potential for growth and expansion of consciousness. It is all up to us!

Unfriendly Force

There is not much difference in dealing with an unfriendly force, whether it comes to us from outer space or from an unfriendly person that we meet in our earthly travels. In either case, the creativity that normally helps us manifest what we want and need is somehow being misqualified, and we are being forced to address issues in our life of which we were previously unaware.

Until this happens, most people are unaware that we are multi-dimensional Beings. Ordinarily, on an energetic level, many things are happening that support even the mundane functions of life. The energies behind the scene are very complex. Our physical world is energy too.

The primary factors are whether our thoughts are life-affirming and our feeling-base is uplifting, or whether we are operating from some other combination. It may be unpleasant to discover how our thoughts and feelings have attracted the life circumstances that we have.

If it so happens that another Being has pushed down on our astral body, trying to get in, it is helpful to view the Violet Light of God coming to us from deeper levels within our heart where we connect with God. After this Violet Light has built up, we can visually burst open—*whoosh*—and let the Violet Light fill the other Being. This forces the other Being to deal with his/her own issues.

On another level, the unfriendly force may have created an energetic line or "cord" to us for their own purposes. If we use our imagination to allow us to have "inner vision" in our mind's eye, we may see this cord from another person to ourselves. We experience this through our third-eye vision, similar to how we see in our dreams.

Actually, it is normal to form cords with other people that we like or people we love. It means that we are sharing at certain energy levels with other people. This is much different from an unfriendly force that has another agenda and is tapping into us.

It is interesting to note that when our energy is going out to another, we may feel tired and drained. When their energy is coming in to us, we may become irritable or angry when we seemingly have no reason for feeling that way. What we find is that, just like in our physical life, we can and must establish energetic boundaries with ourselves and with others.

If someone else can imagine cords in order to attach to us then we can imagine cutting those cords with scissors or our blue sword of personal empowerment. Eventually we learn that we can imagine a Sacred Space around us that is positive and promotes our highest and best interests for our expression. This space helps to empower us.

It is helpful to imagine all the other aspects of our life the way we want them to fit together, and to feel excited that they are happening the way we want! We are in harmony with Spirit and the universe, and living our higher purpose.

As we focus on being our most loving expression, we inherently receive protection with it. While positive energy and positive direction are taking place, there isn't any room left within for subversive forces to operate.

Worrying and investigating for possible intruders tends to be counter-productive since our focus is what creates our positive reality. We learn to hold our focus on positive expression. We learn that what we imagine then becomes real in the physical world. If you can see yourself doing something, then you are half the way toward manifesting it.

There is one very important point to remember. If a Being is intruding on our space and we try to push them out, it becomes a power struggle. We may instead focus on our connection with God and our positive direction that is past all interference. Our energy field and protection builds up and we are empowered. We then enter a state of grace.

I will share with you an expression from the late Lorraine Rutherham. She was a friend and a gifted psychic from Denver. She said:

*"Dreamweaver, Dreamweaver
weave your own Dreams, or . . .
Someone else will weave you into Theirs!"*

Manifesting our Heart's Desire

Energy is operating behind the scenes and within everything that is created. Before meditation and spiritual prayer, we learned that if we put out a strong desire to the universe for things, along with a positive mental attitude, that these things would have a tendency to show up in our life. Strong beliefs and faith have a positive effect.

Conversely, a bad past experience that carries a strong emotional charge creates the same kind of experience to come back into our life again. It seems that being determined not to make that mistake again only makes it happen that much faster—very frustrating. Judgments and strong opinions have a tendency to bring experiences around again for us to learn to let go.

Coming from a place of jealously or resentment toward others, or low self-esteem for ourselves, only attracts punishment into our lives. These experiences are so painful that they make us want to let go of them as soon as possible. This is the basis for emotional release processing. Light dissolves emotional heaviness.

Prayer to control others always comes back to us karmically, no matter how badly we think someone needs it. We pray for the *situation* to have the best possible outcome. We pray to empower others to empower themselves.

These principles are behind our prayers, putting magic into our life. We know how much better things happen in our life when we are in the flow. We notice how synchronicities occur when we are aligned with Spirit and in gratitude. Our needs are satisfied and the universe responds to our desires. We are blessed!

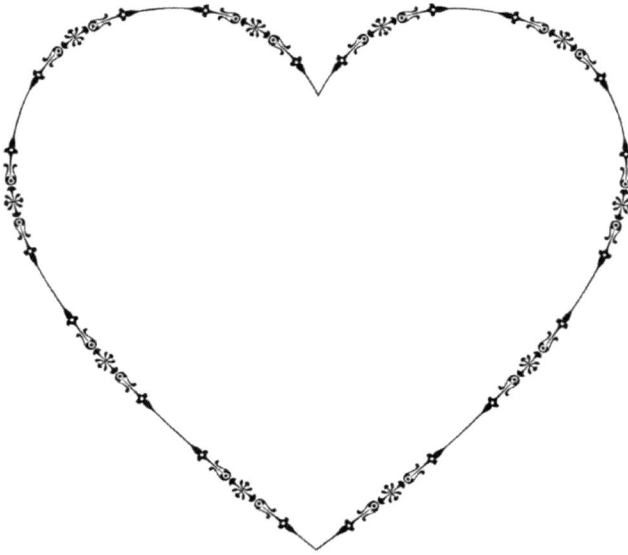

---◆---

The Prayer

Gratitude and Celebration
of Manifesting our Heart's Desire

(to be spoken aloud)

We give thanks in prayer. We celebrate our expression and opportunity to grow. We celebrate the sharing of joy and the flow of love through our lives. We thank you Father and Mother God, a loving universe, and a loving Mother Earth for all the blessings that are bestowed upon us.

We are thankful for helping us to see the beauty, the joy, and the Light in all of creation, and to see the Light burning brightly within.

We are thankful for helping us to lift up our awareness. Through our alignment with Spirit and higher purpose, we raise our sense of oneness with all creation.

We thank you for giving us a glimpse of the wonder of Spirit. We have appreciation for our unlimited expression and ever-expanding truth.

Our hearts open in appreciation as we move into a state of Grace. Our lives are an extension of the love and deeper truth of our Being.

As we open to receive, we are increasingly aware of the great nurturing and support of the universe.

In a place of innocence and alignment with God, all that is required are our desire and our passion!

Thank you, God! Thank you, Guidance! Thank you, Angels!

Amen, Amen, and Amen

---◆---

The Nature of Spiritual Reality

The keys to understanding Spiritual reality lie in the different levels of consciousness and the different levels of awareness. Many times, we think we see things clearly, only to find out later that we were caught up in certain levels of distortion. What we thought was a change in outside reality ultimately turns out to be a change in our inner awareness and understanding.

In the book *Autobiography of a Yogi,* Yogananda reaches a point of enlightenment where he has a sudden realization that there is nothing outside of ourselves except what we are creating from the inside. God does indeed create everything, but the way it is done is to energize or empower the thoughts and feelings of creation. That is how we in humanity maintain "free will" and still have our prayers answered.

To the degree that our passion and our thoughts align with the purposes of higher expression, the intelligence and Love of God can flow through us to create miracles, yet also allow us to experience what happens in a lesser degree of alignment. "Free will" also allows us to experience the results of creating our realities on our own without alignment.

It is also good to know that prayers in Christ consciousness and meditation with higher Light can elevate us to align with the higher purpose of our expression.

I was fortunate enough to experience this same type of awareness on a spiritual quest to Sedona, Arizona. I had traveled there to practice the facilitation of spiritual healing, and to learn and grow. I felt I was guided to go there. It was a Spirit Quest, and it was a great adventure!

The energies are known to be high in Sedona, with energy vortexes exaggerating the processes of creating our realities. The higher purpose of the vortexes is most likely to keep Mother Earth in balance with the constantly changing need for energy and stabilization.

A side benefit for visitors seeking adventure is that the high energies help us to see the results of exaggerated realities that change with our every whim.

After visiting with friends at a coffee house one day, I was told by several people, independently, that I was not in Sedona for the people, but rather I was there to anchor Light in service to God and for the benefit of the area.

I returned to my personal space, which I called *Angels Grace Healing Ministry*. After meditating for a while and asking God why I had been drawn to the area, I remembered the story I had been told several months before. A gentleman watching a store told me that Sedona was a magical home base, but that for money he took groups on sacred tours to experience other places in the world. He said that when he traveled to a new area, the first thing he would do is to meditate with the area and connect into the new place—or "ground in" at the new location.

I remembered him saying that, so I decided to do the same thing. I connected with the Sedona area and "grounded in" to that location. I was looking for answers.

I then went back to the coffee shop to visit with others again, and I noticed a great change. Several people told me, unsolicited, that I was there for "the people" and that I had been drawn to the area in service for the people there. This was a dramatic change from what I had been told several hours earlier!

By the way, everyone in Sedona feels that s/he is a psychic. The energies are very strong.

I went back to meditate again and I had a sudden flash of insight, just like Yogananda. I could see that whatever I was thinking was creating a new scenario for my life and all the supporting circumstances would instantly change. What a realization that was for me! I realized that the universe does truly reflect our view of reality, and that if we change our view, our confirmations in the physical instantly change as well. I had a vision of vast open space around me filled with opportunity and in readiness to create another reality. I realized that everything is an illusion that someone somewhere has created from thought with passion and with purpose.

A friend had an opportunity to have an audience with Sai Baba. When she walked in to visit he said, "I am God . . . and you are God! The only difference between you and me is that I know who I am and you don't!" This was a startling announcement. Before she left, she asked him what the most important thing was that humanity needed to know. He said, "Humanity needs to know that they are not victims." The messages were abrupt, but they were very clear.

R alph Marston was kind enough to share a message that he published in the *Daily Motivator*. I have included it here to bring these thoughts into focus and to plant seeds for everyone who wants to seek truth and understanding.

The Daily Motivator

Thursday, February 8, 2007

-----A positive light-----[1]

Every fear you feel is coming from you. All your thoughts of negativity are being created in your own mind.

And because of that, you can be free of them. For it is you who ultimately decides where your mind will go and what it will hold.

Your thoughts are not caused by anything outside of you. They are the result of the way you've chosen to respond to life.

If your thoughts seem to be holding you prisoner, remember that those thoughts are of your own choosing. You can always at any time make a different choice.

Simply imagine being free of your fears and suddenly that's precisely where you are. Fill your mind with positive, empowering thoughts and you'll quickly crowd out the thoughts that bring you down.

Reality is as it is and you can choose to see it in any light you wish. Cast a positive light on life and you'll connect yourself with real success.

Living in Higher Consciousness

*A*s we grow and evolve, many questions arise. How can we put our making money into synchronicity with our spiritual truth? How do we make time for raising a family with conscious awareness, and at the same time find balance with our path of service and personal fulfillment? How can we be in harmony and be happy?

The answers to all our questions can be found when we look at life through the different dimensions. This is a part of the higher awareness for which we strive.

On a mundane and practical level, we have all become accustomed to business as usual with certain rules of expectation. Favors are returned. Teachers are paid to teach. Service occupations are compensated using the computerized list and the appropriate fee schedule. Housing has certain expectations for rent. Transportation has varying cost expectations and varying dependability.

As we move to higher levels of awareness, the rules of operation start to change. If we put our effort forward in service for someone's benefit, things do return to us—perhaps from that person, or perhaps through someone else or some other avenue of life's expression. It will return to us through the right timing that is advantageous for the forces of Love to move forward. The positive actualizing of Love energy occurs in Spirit's timing at the right hour, at the right place, and in the right way—and not necessarily when we expect or want things to happen.

If we live in trust and in positive expectation, Spirit takes what we need or want into the equation and provides for us. This is a bigger picture than it first appears, because it includes personal needs in the best way and at the best time. It includes guidance for our personal growth and lessons in understanding. Many times, our situations are stressful because we do not understand the challenges before us. In hindsight, it is much easier to see what the tests are really about, more clearly. Then we can see the levels of support we have in Spirit. This also includes higher purpose and higher expression.

We find that if we lose our patience, it's like telling the energetic universe that we don't trust the process. Our judgments create and lock us into our control issues. If we make judgments about people, things, or situations, we then must deal with those things later as if they were really so. In this way, we structure our reality for us to deal with. We find that the universe is responsive to our present positive thoughts and feelings, as well as to the whole gambit of memories of our past experiences and our interpretations thereof, whether positive or not.

Many of us have experience with different techniques for the release of heavy emotions. Meditation and spiritual practices bring more focus into our spiritual views and our personal connection with God. New understandings raise our levels of awareness.

Albert Einstein said that, "no problem can be solved from the same level of consciousness that created it." Perhaps these problems create the situations in life for our continual growth and evolution. In any case, this provides a key for putting our lives together so they will work in harmony.

Our spiritual practices and meditations bring higher awareness to our lives on all levels—from service to the Light and benefiting humanity, to providing support for family, to sharing family love and emotional closeness, to management for everyone's physical well-being. Whether it is for a family or for an individual, it is still best to honor every person in balance with ourselves.

Our process may begin with honoring ourselves and aligning ourselves with higher Light and higher awareness. As we bring Light into our lives, the problems begin to dissolve, and our reality begins to shift to a kinder, more accommodating experience. This higher Light permeates all aspects of life—from business, social, romantic, and spiritual aspects, as well as supporting our personal path. Areas that once seemed in conflict magically adjust themselves into greater harmony and balance.

In situations of great diversity in the family, honoring each individual may entail stronger boundaries for everyone to coexist together.

This dissemination of higher Light and consciousness changes the appearance of all things and all situations to be "lighter." We may purposefully bring more Light into our lives and live with excited anticipation to see how our prayers are answered.

With more Light coming into our lives, and with ever-changing circumstances to deal with, it is crucial to monitor our status on different levels as we go. This enables us to receive new spiritual insight in all aspects of our lives. It enables us to maintain clarity and balance. Always pray for Spirit to "show us how it works" in our lives.

In Love and Light, Namasté

The Rosary

The Lord's Prayer . . . *Aramaic translation or your own (note: idioms/double meanings)*

"Father in heaven, Sanctified be thy Name. Let thy Kingdom come. Let thy Will be done, as above so upon earth. Keep giving us the bread (*teaching*) we need from day to day, and forgive us our debts (*sins*) as we also forgive everyone indebted to us. Let us not enter into the test (*wrongful thinking*), but deliver us from evil (*wickedness, mistake*) for Thine is the Kingdom and the Power and the Glory forever and ever. Amen, Amen, and Amen"[2]

Glory be to the Father, and to the Son, and to the Holy Spirit; as it was in the beginning, is now, and ever shall be, world without end. Amen, Amen, and Amen

Hail Mary, full of Grace, the Lord is with thee! Blessed art thou amongst women, blessed is the fruit of thy womb, Jesus. Holy Mary, Mother of God, pray for us now, the hour of our death, and forever. Amen, Amen, and Amen

Apostles' Creed. I believe in one God, the Father Almighty, Creator of heaven and earth; and in Jesus Christ, His only Son, our Lord; who was conceived by the Holy Spirit, born of the Virgin Mary, suffered under Pontius Pilate, was crucified, died and was buried. He descended into hell. On the third day, He rose again from the dead. He ascended into heaven, and sitteth at the right hand of God, the Father Almighty. From thence shall He come to judge the living and the dead. I believe in one God. I believe in the Holy Spirit. I believe in miracles. I believe my prayers are heard and answered. I believe in the communion of saints, the forgiveness of sins, the resurrection of the body, and life everlasting through the Sacred Heart of Jesus Christ, the Holy Spirit of God and Mary Mother of our Lord and Savior, Mary Queen of peace. Amen, Amen, and Amen

The Devotion of the Rosary

1 **Sign of the cross and Apostles' Creed** - Holding the Crucifix, make the sign of the cross while saying "In the name of the Father, Son, and Holy Spirit," then say the Apostles' Creed

2 **The Lord's Prayer** - Moving up to hold the single bead just above the cross, say the Lord's Prayer

3 **Hail Mary** - On the next cluster of three beads, say the Hail Mary (one time per each bead)

4 **Glory be** - On the chain or cord after the three beads, say the Glory be

5 **The Lord's Prayer** - On the next bead, say the Lord's Prayer

6 **Hail Mary** - On the first set of ten beads of the Rosary, say the Hail Mary (one time per each bead)

7 **Glory be and The Lord's Prayer** - On the next bead say both the Glory be and the Lord's Prayer

8 **Hail Mary** - On the second set of ten beads of the Rosary, say the Hail Mary (one time per each bead)

9 **Glory be and The Lord's Prayer** - On the next bead say both the Glory be and the Lord's Prayer

10 **Hail Mary** - On the third set of ten beads of the Rosary, say the Hail Mary (one time per each bead)

11 **Glory be and The Lord's Prayer** - On the next bead say both the Glory be and the Lord's Prayer

12 **Hail Mary** - On the fourth set of ten beads of the Rosary, say the Hail Mary (one time per each bead)

13 **Glory be and The Lord's Prayer** - On the next bead say both the Glory be and the Lord's Prayer

14 **Hail Mary** - On the fifth set of ten beads of the Rosary, say the Hail Mary (one time per each bead)

15 **Glory be and The Lord's Prayer** - To close at the end of the Rosary, say the Glory be and the Lord's Prayer, both on the last bead.

Mary's message to us, "Pray the Rosary"

NOTES:

The Lord's Prayer can be used by itself in times of need to bring ourselves closer to God. As a meditation, it fills us with Light.

See also the Ten Commandments given to Moses after he led his people out of slavery in Egypt. Deuteronomy Chapter 5: verses 7-21. It is also found in Exodus Chapter 20: verses 3-17.

See also the Beatitudes, Matthew 3: verses 5-10

[2]"The Lord's Prayer" by Jack Kilmon reproduced by permission.

Blessings from the Dolphins

I was walking in my living room one day in Lakewood, Colorado. I was meditating on lots of healing and teaching topics and I started wondering what the dolphin energy feels like. Suddenly the energy came in! After several months, I went to a metaphysical fair and offered to bring in the dolphin energy to someone. She channeled for me the following message from a dolphin by the name of "Voice of the Waves." She said his colors were blue and silver.

"I am a voice
laughing in the waves,

Come ride with me
to a secret cave,

Feel the cool and
rush of the sea,

Riding, laughing,
sing with me,

Crystal,
coral gems of the sea,

I am here,
come back and swim with me!"

- Voice of the Waves

Reflections on Life

We look to Spirit rather than to individuals. Our expectations are too big to be met by any one individual. We pray to Spirit for what we need.

Help comes through many, and takes the best available avenue. We look to Spirit to see how our prayers are being answered.

We empower everyone's ability to empower themselves. We each have guides and challenges to solve. We each have trust, faith, and sincerity with which to work.

If we rescue someone from their lessons, they will have to re-create new learning situations, and in the meantime, we're caught up in the drama again. We learn not to rescue, but rather assist.

Relationships begin with biological attraction. They test our resolve and our patience. To last, we need to be lifted by Holy Spirit and Light in peace and harmony with purpose in common.

Hanging onto harsh experiences tells the Universe that we haven't yet learned to let go, and that we may need more similar experiences before we can grow.

We plant seeds of desire and have faith in the best. Spirit empowers our prayers and strengthens the rest of life relationships, health, and success. Light fills the cycles of life and our expectations.

First, we think, feel, and know life is good, and then we get confirmation that this is so.

**We think life is gloomy,
Or we think life is bright,
Either way that we see it,
We prove we are right.**

Formula Rub

In large container, add together and shake:

32 ounces Wintergreen rubbing alcohol
1 cup White Sage
½ cup Sea Salt (add with left hand)
1 clove of Garlic
1 Penny
1 teaspoon of Coca Cola

Let sit in sun all day. Can be used after sunset.

This is for external use only!

This is a home remedy formula for energy release. The purpose is to rub it on the skin and draw out the negative energies while raising one's vibration rate. A good friend who was a Native American Indian from the Apache Tribe and a dedicated healer gave this recipe to me many moons ago.

This works to raise vibrations, but please check with your guidance and your healthcare professional before use.

The more we practice,
The better we get at it!

- John Pollock

V
AFFIRMATIONS AND INVOCATIONS

This chapter contains affirmations and invocations for purposes of support, and ends with a letter and prayer to the universe in which we can all participate for World Peace.

A **PRAYER** is a request for assistance from Spirit.

An **INVOCATION** is a call to the energies of Spirit to become active within us.

An **AFFIRMATION** is a prayer stated as if the desired manifestation is already complete.

NOTE:
When saying an affirmation,
it is best to repeat the entire affirmation
three times aloud.

---◆---

Universal Prayer
Original 1945 version by Alice A. Bailey & Djwhal Khul
(public domain)

The Great Invocation

From the point of Light within the Mind of God
Let Light stream forth into the minds of men.
Let Light descend on Earth.

From the point of Love within the Heart of God
Let Love stream forth into the hearts of men.
May Christ return to Earth.

From the centre where the will of God is known
Let purpose guide the little wills of men -
The purpose which the Masters know and serve.

From the centre which we call the race of men
Let the Plan of Love and Light work out.
And may it seal the door where evil dwells.

Let Light and Love and Power
restore the Plan on Earth.

---◆---

Invocations to Center

The following are three different invocations to choose from to come into center and alignment with Spirit. What is important is to use the prayer that resonates and works best with us.

I invoke the Light of Christ within me,
I am aligned with my Higher Light,
I am grounded in the Holy Spirit,
I am in perfect flow with myself and the universe,
I am a clear and perfect channel of Light,
Light is my guide.

> *- author unknown*

I am Light,
I am Love,
I am Divine will,
I am perfect design,
I am aligned!

> *- author unknown*

We call ourselves to center and to ground.
We call our truth forward from within our heart
into perfect alignment with Spirit,
through soul and higher self,
through Divine Father and Mother God,
to the purest heart of Love and Light of all Creation and All That Is!

L et's sit for a moment and see if what we are feeling has changed. It may be very subtle. Notice a feeling of well-being or a fine tingling sensation in the crown. It may be like bringing in more awareness around us. We may feel space or we may feel more at peace or a feeling of well-being.

Although we all experience energy differently, what we're experiencing right now is what we want to look for in the future. We want to use a centering and grounding process to feel this way again. Then we can help others.

Next is our invocation to ground. It involves calling all of the parts of ourselves to come forward connecting with Mother Earth for grounding and healing and balance. Grounding is necessary for us to remember our meditations and to carry out practical expression of Spirit in our lives.

Visualization and Invocation
to Ground

When we visualize we are in the forest by a stream and feeling that we are at one with nature, it works well, but under stress, it may be difficult to stay focused. The following is a visualization and invocation for grounding that works very well under *all* conditions.

Visualization to Ground:

Visualize a "tail" coming down out of our spine and wrapping around an axis at the center of Mother Earth. This works well. We can also visualize a funnel coming from our base chakra, opening downward and connecting with Mother Earth. We might "flash" down and connect. This has the advantage of keeping us free from interference and making a strong connection at the same time.

Feel the energy surging up through us and expanding as we connect to Mother Earth. With Her assistance, we tap into Mother Earth for nurturing and support, filling every chakra and moving upward. See our aura expanding around us as we charge our energy field for protection and empowerment!

Invocation to Ground:

We call ourselves to ground!

We call all aspects of ourselves forward that

resonate with Mother Earth . . .

We ask Her to come forward and connect with us

in grounding, healing, balance, nurturing, and support.

Amen, Amen, and Amen

Feel the change in our energy and well-being!

I would like all of us to bring our attention to our feet. See if we notice vibration in our feet, or a tingling sensation. We may feel heat. If so, that's a sign that Mother Earth energies are connecting with us. If we don't have those familiar sensations, then we're not grounded yet. We all have our own way of telling, but when we can feel those familiar signs again, then we know we are grounded. When grounded, we feel more present and able to perform practical aspects of living while at the same time being connected with guidance. It's very practical to be grounded.

Invocation to the Holy of Holies

Center and ground before beginning. This is a very spiritual invocation. It refers to the Holy of Holies. It is the innermost part of the Jewish Tabernacle, the Sacred Temple where the Ark of the Covenant was kept in Jerusalem. The focus is on bringing in Light and raising our vibration rate as well as bringing ourselves into alignment to accept Light. This also works well to call in our space brothers that are in the Light.

> I call to the Holy of Holies,
>> Kadosh, Kadosh, Kadosh, Adonai,
>> Adonai Sabaoth!
> Holy, Holy, Holy, Lord God of Hosts
>> Praise God heaven and earth
>> Praise God most high!
>
>> Amen, Amen, and Amen

Hebrew Invocation to God (public domain)

PRONUNCIATION GUIDE:
"Kadosh" is pronounced **KAH-DŌSH'**
"Adonai" is pronounced **Ă DŌ-NĪ'**
"Sabaoth" is pronounced **SAH-BAH-ŌTH'**

Affirmation Prayers

O n another level, it is helpful to use positive affirmations for staying in our flow. They are similar to positive motivational programming except we connect with Spirit to make them into prayers as well. We also can meditate with guidance and create affirmations as prayers to suit our personal needs. Positive subconscious reprogramming is very important to keep us on track during times when we're distracted and not consciously steering our life.

The following are examples of personal affirmations. It is most important, however, that we all create affirmations for ourselves. To do that, I am sharing the following exercise:

1. We call ourselves into Center, Alignment on all levels, and Ground.

2. We write down on a piece of paper the things in our lives that we want to change.

3. We turn the paper over and re-write these into "I AM" statements.

Note: It's important for us to follow through with this in order to support our path.

One of the most important things to discuss here is the balance of male and female energies inside us. We all have both male and female energies within us. When things aren't working in our lives, we are usually imbalanced energetically. Ideally, it would be good if concern for our feelings and well-being from the feminine side were in balance with the masculine side of action we are taking to meet our personal goals.

Our personal empowerment is heavily dependent upon a strong recognition and alignment of our feminine side. When we are out of balance, we are usually operating strictly on masculine energy. The things that we want to do may not be happening the way that we want, so we tend to work harder to make things happen. That still doesn't work. We are sacrificing our feelings of well-being and our appreciation of our self in order to put more effort into overcoming whatever obstacles seem to be in the way of moving ahead.

Situations don't usually turn around until we start doing the things that promote our feeling better—getting enough sleep, taking time to appreciate life, meditating to release stress, and connecting with guidance. These things are uplifting. These things help us to feel better about life and our self. These kinds of activities help us to get back in touch with our feminine side and restore personal balance.

In addition to nurturing ourselves, we can invoke feminine energies from Spirit to channel through us. This strengthens our awareness of our feminine side. If we invoke

Divine Mother, Quan Yin, Mother Mary, Archangel Uriel, or even Mother Earth, we reinforce our feminine side even more. This also brings more Light into our lives for living and healing. Empowerment through our feminine side then attracts the people, places, and situations to us for our lives to start working again. This is the perfect balance to go along with our spiritual guidance.

Besides bringing ourselves to balance and empowerment with Spirit, it is best to recall past experiences with positive results, and bring those feelings of confidence and success forward in our memory. It helps to see and feel this past success as confirmation for our flow of success and for it to continue. This also helps to reinforce our faith and trust.

For those of us who have not had a record of success in any area of our lives, we must develop a "try and try again" approach until we start seeing the confirmation that we want. We must also be flexible and unattached to the outcome, especially while we develop our expectation of success.

It's nice to continually remind ourselves that in the past we had the inner power with Spirit to create the reality that we have now. This is not to blame ourselves, but to understand that we also have the power to create a *new* reality if we so choose, and we always have free choice. It's a matter of choice and a matter of practice.

If we're not getting the results that we want, it's a good idea to look inside. We may have a tendency to blame others rather than to look inside for our own issues. Holding harsh judgments against life or carrying heavy emotions can hold us back. Once we realize it is our own outlook that makes all the difference, then we begin to let a loving universe reflect our love back to us.

We are better served to focus on fulfillment and success rather than old problem situations. We must be in the present, in the flow and flexible, and allow things to come about in "right order." We create a Sacred Space with Spirit, consciously align and balance, and do it often. We choose to have success and fulfillment. Set goals, make plans for success, and keep a positive frame of mind.

Our empowerment relies heavily on being balanced in our feminine side. We nurture ourselves and know that we are always supported. Continually ask guidance for our highest good, where to go, what to do, for assistance in our alignment, nurturing our soul, and bringing us peace.

Finally, and once again with gratitude, say this powerful prayer to the universe, *"We know we are supported . . . universe show us how!"* Then expect the unexpected!

REMEMBER!
When saying an affirmation,
it is best to repeat the entire affirmation
three times aloud.

Personal Affirmation

I am healthy, happy, whole, and balanced,
I am happy and harmonious in all my relationships,
I am prosperous and in complete attunement with the Light,
I am free to do and be who I am without restriction,
I am loved with universal love, I fear not,
We thank you Father for all the blessings you have bestowed upon us,
And for allowing us to be in service to the Light!

Support Affirmation

This is not a problem no matter how it looks,
No matter what's in progress,
I don't have to "create" a problem out of this!
I take a deep breath . . .
I let stress go, let drama go,
I create a new adventure,
I choose a new adventure!
I know I'm always supported,
Universe, show me how!

In the name of Lord Jesus Christ,
Amen, Amen, Amen, and so it is!

Affirmation for Attracting Enlightened Relationships

We attract Divinely Right relationships through Love.

The exchanges will raise our level of consciousness and be uplifting.

In romance, our relationships are sharing and beneficial for us both, bringing joy and fulfillment.

We call for Light to anchor within us, expanding our expression and service to the Light.

We experience how well relationships can work through grace and compassion.

Our dance with life is filled with Light and joy in each new adventure!

Amen, Amen, and Amen

Reference: Ester and Jerry Hicks general information.
www.moneyandthelawofattraction.com

Affirmations for Order and Prosperity

This affirmation is to be used in times of overwhelm. The same principle applies in other places. This is for when the telephone is ringing and everyone seems to be demanding too much time, and when everyone seems to want meetings at the same time. This also works for bill collectors calling at the same time, or when you are a supplier and everyone seems to demand your services yesterday. This calls for a change in mindset. Watch your schedule open up! Take several deep breaths . . .

Affirmation: Everything is in Order

Everything is in order through Light.
I have time for everyone,
and resources for completion.
I am in sync with Universal flow.
I am balanced!

This affirmation is to be used with the understanding that these blessings already exist in our lives, and that we must place ourselves in the Light of Gratitude while affirming these blessings so that they may increase and multiply.

Affirmation for Prosperity[3]

What's mine is mine
through Divine design,
In a perfect way
on this perfect day!

[3]Reprinted with permission from Ms. Ann Swenson, Colorado Springs, Colorado

Affirmation for Empowerment and Magnificence

The Love of God resides within,
The Power of God radiates,
The Intelligence of God creates,
The Light of God illuminates,
Peace, joy, and harmony abide within!

Affirmation for Realization

What we seek is here
In Divine order
In perfect timing
Through perfect Love!

We know and See the truth . . .
What we seek is already here!

Affirmations for Empowerment

These affirmations and decrees are very powerful. They work well in times of overwhelm. The Violet Flame is God's energy of freedom and transformation. It dispels all fear and desperation.

Light, Light, Light!
Expanding
Enlightening
Empowering . . .
Now and forever!

* * *

The power of God dwells within, it . . .
Consumes heaviness
Leads past interference
Overcomes obstacles
Inspires me
It shows me the way!

* * *

I am the Flame of Violet Fire
Purifying, Raising, Higher and Higher!

Affirmation for Abandonment Issues

The solution for abandonment issues is to fill the hole in our heart with ourselves. If we look outside of ourselves, it will never be enough. When heartache strikes, we bring our attention to the painful feelings. We tune into Holy Spirit for healing, and say to ourselves:

I fill the hole in my heart with myself.
I am here for myself.
I no longer need anyone else to make me whole or happy.

I am whole and complete and I accept full healing from God.
I feel the warmth in my heart.
I am one with Spirit!

Thank You, God
Amen, Amen, and Amen

Affirmations for Conflict Resolution

Years ago when I was visiting Sedona, Arizona, there was a rough and tumble guy who caused quite a stir in town. His name was "Ed the Waver." He traveled the roads and highways on foot, always waving at traffic driving by. He felt it was his calling.

Some people thought that was great. Some people were outraged, "Who does he think he is, always waving like that?" In any case, he had many experiences and many stories and he shared some with us.

He was in jail overnight on a misunderstanding for trying to break up a fight and stop a riot from occurring. While he was there, he shared a cell with a particularly large and imposing inmate. They were both waiting to see the judge. At first, Ed felt intimidated but then realized the man was afraid of being found guilty for the third time and sent to jail with no possibility of parole.

Ed shared some sage advice with the man going before the judge. The judge asked the man if he was serious about changing his life. The judge then let the man go with a warning, saying he didn't want to see him in that courtroom again! This was contrary to his reputation as a tough judge.

To make the story short, below is the affirmation that Ed recommended. This affirmation can be used by all of us when facing conflict-resolution situations!

Only love and understanding fills my heart!

Only love and understanding fills his heart!

Only love and understanding fills our hearts!

This may seem too simple, but try this the next time you find yourself in a difficult situation and you will experience the power of the words.

Affirmation to Prevent Interference

This affirmation is used to prevent interference from dark-side, unfriendly entities, or other people.

I give you no fear, I give you no anger; therefore you have no power over me! I give you only Love and Light![4]

I align with Light from above and Earth below anchoring into my heart. I create a Sacred Space with Light flowing around and through me. As a Light-worker I am already anchoring Light. This is a reminder to anchor more Light and accept it for myself.

I focus past would-be distractions and obstacles, and only go in the direction I choose to go. I focus on the positive and uplifting in the present, yet I remain vigilant. I raise all consciousness and misqualified energies to the Highest and release them to the Light to be healed in Divine Right Action.

I refer difficult situations to Archangel Michael and the Ashtar Command[5] *to be resolved in the Light! I give thanks for insight and support in all things!*

Amen, Amen, and Amen

<u>Note:</u> Engaging energies that would threaten us only empowers the struggle. Anchoring a Sacred Space and holding a strong focus on our higher path inherently includes protection while assisting us with guidance, direction, and healing. Many times this is a lesson in trust and holding our own alignment with Spirit. We release fear and experience the quiet power of Love and Light empowering our lives.

[4]Used with permission from Ms. Judy Edmondson, Lakewood, Colorado
[5]The Ashtar Command is the enforcement branch of the Light

Build Your Own Affirmation

Step 1

Meditate on what your needs are on all levels from the mundane—money, family, social relationships—to your spiritual path. Acknowledge all gifts provided to you and ask for new gifts to handle the service that you want to provide for others. Make a list.

Step 2

Put the list into a positive statement using the phrase "I am . . ." This puts the affirmation into the present tense and presents it as already completed energetically, as far as the universe is concerned.

Step 3

Tell Spirit what you will do in service to the Light should your requests be granted. Release all roadblocks to Spirit. Then release your requests in an energetic ceremony to be fulfilled! Be as extravagant as you wish. Try this and see the many interesting things that happen. Report back!

Invocation Prayer
in Service as Facilitator
(Prayers for channeling, healing, and counseling)

This invocation can be modified to suit many different uses. This is a basic framework from which to create your own prayers. It is set up now for healing work.

I call myself to center and to ground.

I release myself in service to the Light for the Highest and best use for each person involved.

I call to each person's personal guides, the Archangels, the Sacred Energies, Christ Holy Spirit, Mother Earth, and the highest alignment possible with God.

I hold a loving, neutral space without limitation! (This is the most powerful healing position the facilitator can take.)

I release this healing session to Spirit for guidance and direction for the Highest Good.

Amen, Amen, and Amen

Prayer and Vision for World Peace

In such fast changing times, the question arises from time to time as to our well-being in the world. I am therefore putting forth this letter to Spirit in Universal Prayer.

I invite everyone to make these prayers their own. If we look closely, we can see miracles unfolding every day! To the Glory of God for the benefit of humankind and a precious Mother Earth, we accept this happening! May this prayer be passed on to others. May we see the blessings of Love and Light continue to mount and unfold!

By all that is Holy, so may it be!

---◆---

The Prayer
World Peace
(to be spoken aloud)

I see all of us praying each in our own way for inspiration and the power of Love and Light to touch the hearts of humankind.

On a personal level, I see widespread recognition and empowerment of ourselves, nurturing and accepting the unlimited potential of God acting through us blessing everyone.

Nationally, I see the best possible leadership guided through Love and Light. I see new opportunities and vision opening up for world leadership with global advancement, harmony, and new solutions for economic disparity.

I see effective conservation becoming a reality. We still have time! I see our delicate balance of ecology restored to health and I see critical damages being repaired.

The very best of humankind often rises out of necessity and I see the best coming forward now. I see us joining around the world in the positive access of new awareness and new solutions!

I see great miracles. I feel the flow of Love and Light through the hearts of humankind. The positive flow is building great momentum now! These miracles are already in progress!

Amen, Amen, and Amen

---◆---

Surrender our will,
Not our joy!

- John Pollock

VI
PRAYERS WITH CEREMONY

This chapter presents prayers and invocations for the use in anchoring Light, aligning ourselves with Spirit, and carrying out our spiritual work.

When we reach the point where we've realized that our prayers for help are actually being answered, it becomes helpful to use certain spiritual tools. We have learned that regular meditation helps us to reconnect to the Light, get new insights, and renew the flow of grace in our lives. It serves us well to do regular ceremony—stabilizing ourselves, holding more Light, and staying in constant communication. Prayers and ceremony help us to work together with the Light for the highest spiritual purpose. Our service is always together with Spirit, acting with guidance, acting in unison, holding Light, and expanding in Love.

This chapter presents prayers and invocations for the use in anchoring Light, aligning ourselves with Spirit, and carrying out our spiritual work.

I Am Aligned

This is a strong prayer acknowledging all things as already done and complete in the present. Within this prayer, we invoke the Rays to open the top four chakras for healing energies to flow unimpeded. Opening and clearing these top four chakras is imperative and very effective for aligning ourselves with Spirit.

---◆---

The Prayer
I Am Aligned
(to be spoken aloud, slowly and clearly)

I am whole and attuned to Spirit on all levels.

I am aligned with Christ Holy Spirit, the Sacred Energies,
and God most High.

I am resonating with the sweet love, nurturing, and support of
Mother Earth.

The Archangels Raphael, Michael, Gabriel, and Uriel bring the four
Sacred Elements.

They hold a Sacred Space.

I am aligned with the . . .

Emerald Green Ray of truth and healing,

Neon Blue Ray of innocence and purification,

White Ray of purity,

Ruby Gold Ray of wisdom.

Pink Unconditional Love blesses my heart.

Neon Blue empowers my expression.

Indigo Light illuminates my vision.

Gold Wisdom brings inspiration and knowledge.

Grace enfolds my life.

Spirit guides my steps.

Thank you, God.

I am Blessed!

---◆---

Free Style Meditation

This is a very simple meditation to connect with the Light. We will automatically have protection and automatically begin clearing. We open ourselves for what Spirit would like to bring to us. This prayer can be for joy and sharing for individuals or groups, and it can be a forum for members to talk on a number of topics. It is for whatever we choose, and it can be a silent or spoken meditation. If it is used in a group setting, we can ask Spirit to guide the meditation for every person's highest good. It would be a good idea to ask for that in any meditation.

We call ourselves to center and to ground.
We call our guides to help anchor a Sacred Space around us.
We open ourselves to the Angels, our teacher guides,
Christ Holy Spirit,
And Mother Earth for nurturing and support and change.
We honor the Sacred Space around us, and we sit with the Light!

Invocation to the Holy Light Within[6]

I Call Forth the Power of Light that I AM

I AM, that I AM, that I AM

I AM, that I AM, that I AM

I AM, that I AM, that I AM

I AM Earth

I AM Air

I AM Fire

I AM Water

I Call to my Teachers and my Guides

I Call to my Higher Self, to the Spirit Essence that I AM

I Call to the Sacred Holy Flames of Light

To the Sacred Violet Flame of Transformation

To the Sacred Emerald Flame of Healing

To the Sacred Pink Flame of Heart

To the Sacred Azure Flame of Cause

I Ask to be Imbued and Blessed with the Energies of Love

And the Sacred Holy Flames of Light

I ask that my Spirit Self, Spirit Guides and Teachers

Assist me to Integrate the Truth of Light that I AM

Beloved I AM

Beloved I AM

Beloved I AM

[6]Used with permission by Athene Raefiel, Colorado
www.atheneraefiel.com

Invocation to the Archangels and Sacred Energies

This invocation is to the Archangels and Sacred Energies. For those not familiar with how to work with the Archangel Energies, we first call ourselves to center and ground, calling to our personal guides and our higher self to connect us with Archangel Michael. We call to Archangel Michael so we can connect to the energies of the other Archangels. Sit in purity of heart with these energies to experience them. Now we are ready to proceed.

After creating a Sacred Space with the Archangels and others, we are ready to use this space for meditation to receive answers, releasing ourselves for service to the Light or commanding Divine Right Action where it is warranted. Use this invocation with discretion and guidance.

We call ourselves to center and to ground.

We call ourselves into perfect alignment with our truth within our heart, the purest heart of Love and Light of all Creation and All That Is.

We call to Mother Earth to connect with us for balance, nurturing, and support.

We call to Archangel Michael and Lady Faith to open and clear our throat chakra,

Archangel Jofiel and Lady Constance to open and clear our crown chakra,

Archangel Chamuel and Lady Charity to open and clear our heart chakra,

Archangel Gabriel and Lady Hope to open and clear our base chakra,

Archangel Raphael and Holy Mother Mary to open and clear our third eye chakra,

Archangel Uriel and Lady Aurora to open and clear our solar plexus chakra, and

Archangel Tzadkiel and Lady Amethyst to open and clear our sacral chakra.

We call to Christ Holy Spirit, the Sacred 104 Lakota energies, the Hermes levels of existence—Source, Aeon, Cosmos, Time, and Genesis on planet Earth—and the Sacred Hebrew Tree of Life levels for creating and manifesting including Emanation, Creation, Formation, and Action.

We call our personal guides and teachers with all these energies to come to us in perfect alignment, for highest and best use, and highest service to the Light!

Amen, Amen, and Amen, and so it is!

Invocation to Create a Sacred Space

This Invocation is more focused and introduces guides and Sacred elements as part of a stronger ceremony of Light. This is a very strong invocation to center and ground. See also the chapter on the "Sacred Medicine Wheel."

We call upon our truth to align our heart with soul, higher self, and the Highest. We resonate with Mother Earth in love and support.

We honor Christ Holy Spirit, the Archangels, the Lakota 104 energies, the Hermes levels of Creation, the Hebrew Tree of Life, and the Great Brotherhood of Light. We call forth the mighty forces of Love and Light to support us and direct us in gaining clarity for our lives and understanding for our challenges.

We call heaven and earth into union of purpose, including the Divas of nature, the Sacred elements of the four directions, and harmony with our personal guides. Our personal growth plays out in harmony with our service to the Light and alignment with the unfolding plans of God, the Universal Spirit of Love and Light.

We unite with the greater purpose of our teachers, guides, angels, and the ascended masters for the highest expression on all levels. Together, we release judgment and blame and move ahead with discernment and compassion. We enter into our highest state of Being.

We unite in Christ Holy Spirit and the Great Brotherhood of Light, in Love and honoring all Life! We are free from struggle and aligned with higher Love.

Amen, Amen, and Amen

And so it is, in Love and Light!

Earth Energy Clearing and Healing

This clearing is necessary to release baggage we carry from past lives, from karma, from stress, hurt, or guilt held energetically in the body. That includes all the things we agreed to feel and release according to our Book of Life—things we agreed to deal with in this lifetime. Sometimes it seems that we can't move ahead until we deal with these certain issues.

As always, remember to ground and center, and establish your Sacred Space with Spirit before performing any healing session or ceremony.

For those first practicing their healing technique: The group or client sits facing South with palms up for sharing information, and the healer faces North with palms down slightly above the client's palms. (In a group, the healer can raise both hands with fingertips pointing toward the sky.)

For more advanced healing practitioners: The facing directions remain the same but the placement of palms and hands may vary according to the best feeling of the practitioner.

THE FACILITATOR SPEAKS:[7]

"See the color blue and water flowing from the hands of the healer.

Release heaviness of organs and sadness held as stress, heaviness of heart. Release past tears that have been trapped.

What is it that you are carrying?

Bring your attention to the discomfort.

Place the issue in your mind's eye. We ask mother earth if she will take it.

Tell her that it serves no purpose any longer and we give permission for her to take it.

We now have windows of opportunity to release baggage and fear-energy from early years.

Olo, come as communicator guide!

Owl energy, come with wisdom!

Healing guides, come with information!

Feel the electricity of North energy coming in.

Feel the flow of water through my hands.

Feel the Light lifting the body as it comes in from Mother Earth.

See blue energy of water flowing through and washing heaviness away.

See the owl with gold feathers sitting on my right shoulder.

Hear the vision that something is releasing.

Hear the sound of water rushing through.

Blow out the breath, and feel the *whoosh* as stress releases!"

[7]Channeled for John in Denver by Andryl Angel, Chris and Bob
www.angelchannel-chrisbob.com/channel.html

Healing Prayer for Transformation

In *A Course in Miracles,* Christ says that if a person wants to change the way s/he thinks all s/he has to do is give those thoughts to Him and He will gradually bend those thoughts around into "perfect order" through grace.

The Prayer
for Transformation
(to be spoken aloud)

We call the highest level of Christ Light forward to fill our Higher Self and Soul. We give any purpose of ourselves that is not of our highest expression over to Christ. We feel those aspects of ourselves going out, and our Being filling with Light.

We call the highest level of Christ Light forward to fill the higher spiritual aspects of ourselves, including our heart. We give our beliefs, our judgments, our mental reality, and our understanding of empowerment to Christ to be reformed. We give our sadness, grief, and hurt to Christ to be replaced with love for everyone, including ourselves. We ask for compassion and discernment for our path. We are open to receive joy and fulfillment. Our heart is blessed.

We call Christ Light forward to fill our solar plexus and mental body. We give our anxieties and our fears to Christ to be uplifted in love. We are open to receive peace and understanding.

We call Christ Light forward to fill our sacral chakra and emotional body. We give our sense of struggle in relationships, money, authority, power, and self-esteem to Christ. We are open to receive feelings of reassurance and single focus.

We call Christ Light forward to fill our base chakra, cell memory, and physical body. We give our stored stress, hurt, anger, self-criticism, and toxicity to Christ for clearing and healing. We are open to be the perfection of love, once again in balance and with renewed life force.

We feel the highest level of Christ Light filling our connection with Mother Earth. We are open to receive grounding, nurturing, and support in a balanced life. We are open for complete healing.

Thank you, Lord, for blessing our soul and our life.

Amen, Amen, and Amen!

Forgiveness Experience
(for processing)

This is a process to bring healing to early childhood experiences, although age is not really a factor. Sometimes the same kind of issues that arise from co-workers and friendships remind us of other experiences. One gender may actually be reminding us of an issue we have with someone else of the opposite gender.

This process can be used as often as necessary, situation by situation.

To begin, visualize yourself surrounded by a circle of Gold Light.

Relax and open your mind. Based on your reflections and internal inventory, pick a situation with which you have some current emotional reactivity. Become aware of any resentment, anger, hurt, pain, or shame that you feel toward the particular person(s) or parent(s) involved. Be specific!

Visualize the person(s) clearly, as if they are sitting in a chair right in front of you. Look at them in the face. See and experience their presence in detail. What are they wearing? What is the expression on their face? What is their posture? What is their attitude? Etc.

Speak directly to the person by saying, "When you did _____ to me, I felt _____." Briefly describe the situation, and most importantly, express your feelings!

Now tell them what you would rather have had them do. "I would have preferred that you _____."

Pause for a few moments after expressing your emotions. Regain a more peaceful, relaxed, centered frame of mind. Take several deep breaths. Now surround both you and the person you have been talking to in a rose-colored light of compassion. Sit peacefully together in the light for a few moments.

When it feels right, say to the person, "I do not want to hold on to my expectations of you to _____. I therefore release you from them with love. I surround us both in the light of compassion and accept us both for who we are. I let go, and let God! I let go of the past and do not need you to be anything or do anything in order for me to be whole and happy. I am willing to be with you in whatever way the universe sees fit."

Now, gently tell the person anything about them that you appreciate, adding "Thank you for allowing me to express my feelings!"

Inspirational Support for Recovery

his prayer is designed for special situations where there is a call for continuous support. From a higher perspective, we may become aware that an addiction forces us to seek help from a higher power in whatever way is appropriate for us. A reoccurring challenge causes us repeatedly to feel the need to reconnect with God, thinking that somehow we've lost our connection. This prayer is to be used on a daily basis or from minute to minute if necessary.

The Prayer
for Continuous Support
(to be spoken aloud)

We call forth our truth from within our heart

To come into perfect alignment with Father and Mother God

Through our soul, higher self, and all aspects of our Being.

Father, please bring us into alignment

For peace, compassion, understanding, forgiveness, and acceptance of the presence of God.

Thank you for the comfort and support coming to us,

And working through us for change.

We release ourselves to you

To show us how healing and transformation may work in our life.

Please direct us to the right places and right people.

May we feel your Presence Most High enter into our physical life.

We accept all blessings and give thanks for this Holy instant.

Amen, Amen, and Amen

Healing Negative Thought Creations

The mental activity of thinking forms the invisible substance of the universe into thought-forms, which then exist and actively influence people, places, and ongoing social interaction. In the positive, they serve us well to manifest and create our lives. In the negative, they work at cross-purposes. They also tend to continue to exist and be active until altered or cancelled by new, positive thoughts of truth and love.

---◆---

The Prayer

Releasing Negatively Influencing Thought-Forms

(to be spoken aloud)

I call to my Highest God Source, my I AM Presence within, and my Holy Christ Self.

I call on the Holy Spirit, spirit of truth and wholeness, to shine the Light of Truth into all negative thought-forms that might influence me adversely. Those misqualified thoughts are now filled with higher Truth and Love, and are dissolved by Divine Light Intelligence.

I release judgment, thoughts of fear, lack, illness, guilt, and blame from my mind as they no longer serve me, and they are now gone. I choose to think new creative thoughts of Light, Truth, Love, Kindness, Peace, Joy, Abundance, and Health for my families and friends, myself, and for humanity.

I am in control of my mind and my focus, both objectively and subjectively.

From my higher truth and alignment with God, I reject all adverse influences, and focus past them to place my focus on my highest expression on all levels.

I choose to be only my highest potential and expression!

I choose to stand in positive alignment and total empowerment!

I thank God that this is now so by decree. So it is!

---◆---

Achieving Integration and Harmony

his is one of the strongest prayers for change. It may bring up issues to work through, yet it can speed up the transformation process. We want to keep this in mind when working through our enlightenment process!

◆

The Prayer
for Integration and Harmony
(to be spoken aloud)

I invoke the Light of Christ within me,

I am grounded in the Holy Spirit,

I am in perfect flow with the universe and myself,

I am a clear and perfect channel of Light,

Light is my guide.

I call all aspects of myself forward into perfect alignment with my truth within my heart, my soul, higher self, and the highest Divine Love and Emanation of God.

I call all aspects of myself forward that resonate with Mother Earth, and ask Her to come forward and connect with me in nurturing, support, and balance.

I choose to move into the Present.

I thank my feminine aspects for nurturing and supporting me, and in balance, I thank my masculine aspects for acquiring necessities and projecting my higher truth in harmony.

Through the grace of God and from my truth within, I call all fragmented aspects of myself to come gently forward at the conscious level and to reveal their feelings and thought patterns. Through higher awareness, I realize that I can move through all issues in this lifetime and lovingly embrace the return of these aspects.

Through conscious choice, I release unwanted drama and need for dysfunction. I release neediness, struggle, and projection of my own judgments; knowing that these affect my own reality. I choose instead to realign with my higher truth and with God.

I allow myself to once again see and feel and know that I am always supported, and ask God to show me how this works.

I move past interference and choose my most loving expression in balance and harmony and joy! I am flowing with a loving universe and expressing my highest potential and highest truth.

All good things come to me in perfect timing and in a perfect way.

God please show me how this is so!

I give thanks to the Highest . . .

Amen, Amen, and Amen

Being in the Flow

The following section is an initiation to being in the flow with the energies of "being love" and bringing these energies into our planet and humanity. We connect with these strong energies and prepare ourselves to live "in the flow," living in the physical world in balance with our higher path. We experience alignment in ceremony and discuss factors that help us to maintain our spiritual connection.

We're in the flow when we notice synchronicity of events. The synchronicity we are speaking of occurs when we are magically in the right place at the right time. This happens when we're living in the present moment, unattached to life circumstances or how our prayers are to be answered. We may still experience emotional trauma, but we choose to ask a loving universe for the highest and best in every situation.

Mother Nature is all Loving and wants to support us. We ask the universe to show us how we are supported. As we release harsh judgments of people and situations, we also release our "make it happen or else" approach. If we are not attached to the outcome, it allows us to receive the highest flow possible. Life becomes a constant surprise!

When our lives are in chaos and we're feeling separation, it is not Spirit that abandons us. We are out of balance. Our guidance and support, however, are always with us. It is up to us to call ourselves back into alignment. When we do this, Love and Light flow through all aspects of our reality bringing joy and fulfillment.

Centering and grounding brings higher Light to balance the energies of lower chakra disturbance. By realigning with nature and Spirit, we move back into our highest and best flow again. This is our celebration of life.

We invoke Great Spirit, Christ Consciousness, and thank Mother Earth for her loving support. This is a quick and effective alignment that can be used when we're feeling off balance in order to create a glorious day or at night to release stress.

We receive these blessings and anchor Light with the following "Invocation of the Elements and Sacred Space":

Invocation of the Elements
and Sacred Space

BEGIN BY FACING THE EAST

From the East we call to the element of Air, to the winds that blow deeply in men's souls—consciousness, insight, birth and rebirth—to what inspires creativity and enlightened understanding.

"We honor you great element, great element of Air.

Inspire our creations with insightfulness and care.

Increase our understanding of all you have to share.

We honor and feel the energies of the East.

Welcome! OM . . ."

TURN TO FACE THE SOUTH

From the South we call to the Fire of Light, to the warmth and the hearth, to the Fire in the sky, igniting our Spiritual Purpose that we may see our path clearly in the Light.

"Great element of Fire, purify now all souls of humankind.

Trial by Fire, transform us with your flame that in rightness we may shine.

We honor and feel the energies from the South.

Welcome! OM . . ."

TURN TO FACE THE WEST

From the West we call to the element of Water—oceans, lakes, and rivers, movement of unconscious mind, and communication within and with the universe.

"Awaken! Awaken! Within all those here,
Communication through consciousness,
The flow of all life, make abundantly clear.
We honor and feel the energies from the West.
Welcome! OM . . ."

TURN TO FACE THE NORTH

From the North we call to the Earth Mother dear, she who clothes and feeds us and nurtures us, holding us near—teaching us practical expression of Spirit.

"Great Mother your magic we wish you unfold
To all within your bosom in this time that's been foretold.
Let us be your great assistants in expansion and Light,
Hold us closely to your heart as we honor you this night.
We honor and feel the energies from the North.
Welcome! OM . . ."

Turn our gaze to Father Sky above

"Great Spirit, Divine Father, and Christ Consciousness above,

Flow down through us; connect our hearts in your Love.

Mother Earth, come up through our feet on this ground,

Anchor deep within our hearts and flow up through the crown.

Complete return to Great Spirit, Divine Father, and Christ Consciousness,

On all levels through this prayer, humanity is divinely blessed. OM . . ."

Next, we become centered and grounded within our Sacred Space. (See Chapter V for "Invocations to Center and Ground") Everybody knows what it is like to feel balanced with nature, then later return to confusion and difficulty. Using these centering and grounding processes, we move out of chaos and into balance. Use these at times that are most difficult. Together we experience and feel our group initiation energies.

As we grow,
the nature of God seems to grow ahead of us,
and with us; and we are a part of it.

- John Pollock

Group Mastermind Manifesting

Whenever two or more people meet in Higher purpose, Spiritual Light joins to lift the meditation. The Light is our new creative partner, referred to as the group "Mastermind." This group "Mastermind" infuses inspiration and empowerment.

The purpose of such a gathering is not to solve each other's problems but rather to establish a conscious connection with Spirit, knowing that the Light is working through us to experience new awareness and increased personal power.

Around the circle, everyone shares positive experiences that have happened since the last gathering, as well as problem areas, needs, and desires they wish to turn over to the Light in prayer during the ceremony.

Problem areas, needs, and desires that a person wishes to remain private do not need to be spoken aloud to still be turned over to the Light in prayer. However, each person *does* write their needs and desires which they wish to manifest, onto a piece of paper for use in the Sharing/Burning part of this Ceremony.

To begin, the facilitator will offer an invocation to set a Sacred Space with Spirit, asking for help from our teachers and guides. The facilitator may begin with something like this and add whatever s/he feels appropriate for the group being directed in this Ceremony on this day:

"We open our heart and soul to Divine Father/Mother God and the Unlimited Light from beyond. We extend our alignment down to Mother Earth with the Spirits of Nature for grounding, stability, balance, nurturing, and support."

Mastermind Principles

1) **ALIGN / SURRENDER** – (all together say) "I AM centered, grounded, and aligned. I surrender to the Light within that I AM."

2) **BELIEVING / UNDERSTANDING** – (all together say) "I AM open to the creative power within me. I AM transformed. My belief systems are expressing my Highest good. I AM empowered. I AM making changes in my life effortlessly."

3) **FORGIVING** – (all together say) "I forgive myself for falling short of my expectations of myself. I forgive my harsh lessons. I forgive situations and people involved. I send love and appreciation to everyone who has taught me that I AM responsible for my own feelings."

4) **VISUALIZATION** – (all together say) "I see a brilliant vortex of Violet Light coming down from the heavens, through the center of our prayer circle, and anchoring below us; bringing Light into our Sacred Space and taking negativity away."

5) **RELEASING** – (all together say) "I release the illusion of limitation. I AM willing to accept the Highest truth about myself."

6) **GRATITUDE** – (all together say) "Rather than doing everything by myself, I know that my life is an extension of Spirit working through me. I AM in gratitude for Spirit. As I focus on the positive workings of Spirit, my life expands even more. I give thanks."

7) **SHARING / BURNING CEREMONY** – (individually each says) "My heart is open. I am growing, becoming, self-actualizing. I AM blessed! I say aloud and burn this manifesting list, releasing it to the Universe . . . Amen."

8) **DEDICATION AND COVENANT** – (all together say) "I dedicate myself to the Highest expression of my Being. I know everything I need comes to me in Divine order, in perfect timing. I go forth with enthusiasm, excitement, and expectancy. I AM."

Instructions for Facilitating

TOGETHER - the group says aloud the first six Affirmations of the Mastermind Principles.

INDIVIDUALLY - each person will offer feedback from the last meeting; then moving in a clockwise circle, each person will say the "Sharing/Burning" statement—Seventh Affirmation of the Mastermind Principles—and burn their petition. Share two or three goals in a positive, present-tense statement—for example: "I AM healthy, I AM successful . . ." The principle is that by asking, a transformation takes place. As we present our goal manifested in the present, we know our difficulties are now solved. We know the Universe energetically supports that. Everyone gives supportive acknowledgment.

TOGETHER - in closing, the group will say the "Dedication and Covenant"—Eighth Affirmation of the Mastermind Principles. This is again confirming our commitment to the Mastermind Principles and to the Light expressing through us.

Seeking Enlightenment

We establish a Sacred Space for participants to experience increased awareness and personal power; to set into motion a process which will assist us to live in harmony with our higher truth.

The purpose here is to set up a process to help us deepen our relationships with God, each in our own way.

The facilitator will offer an invocation to set a Sacred Space with Spirit, asking for help from our Teachers, Guides, Angels, and Ascended Masters.

As a group, we will then say aloud the first eight Principles for Expansion.

We end in silent prayer receiving our own healing and answers in the best way that we can understand and accept them.

Principles for Expansion

1) **Centering and Grounding** – "I call myself to center and alignment with Spirit on all levels. I ask that Mother Earth connect with me with her great love in nurturing and support and healing and balance."

2) **Choice** – "I choose my higher self as the truth of who I AM. I know my higher purpose is the most loving expression of who I AM, creating the highest, and always attracting the best to me."

3) **Setting Intention** – "I set my intention to anchor the flow of Light to Mother Earth in service to the Light for the benefit of humankind and the universe. In return, I receive support and the highest blessings in healing and enlightenment for my own growth."

4) **Invoking Sacred Space** – "I call to the Sacred Elements of Air, Fire, Water, and Earth, along with my Teachers, Guides, Angels, and Ascended Masters to assist me in creating a Sacred Space for prayer."

5) **Surrendering** – "I surrender to the Light within that I AM. I AM experiencing the fine workings of Spirit through me and at the same time, I AM anxiously watching to see what the Light brings to me next!"

6) **Releasing** – "I AM willing to accept the highest truth about myself. I release all harsh thoughts and judgments of others and myself that are not for my highest and best good."

7) **Opening to Receive** – "My heart is open. I AM willing to change, and I AM willing to receive the highest gifts from God for wholeness and growth!"

8) **Gratitude** - "I give thanks for the Light working through my life. I know that I AM supported by Mother Earth and the Universe. I joyously accept abundance and prosperity in perfect time, space, and sequence. I give thanks for all spiritual gifts that help me in my service and expression and physical support."

9) **Silent Prayer** – We listen and watch in anticipation to see how Spirit is answering us. We join in silence.

Freedom Light Meditation

This is a very powerful invocation of Light through the Holy of Holies. We use it in Sacred Ceremonies, as well as to call in star ships of Light and our star brothers and sisters. It is a very Sacred Prayer.

We call forth the mighty forces of Love and Light to support us and direct us in gaining clarity for our lives and understanding for our challenges.

We call heaven and earth into union of purpose, including the Divas of nature, the Sacred elements of the four directions, and harmony with our personal guides.

Our personal growth plays out in harmony with our service to the Light and alignment with the unfolding plans of God/the Universal Spirit of Love and Light.

We unite with the greater purpose of our Teachers, Guides, Angels, and the Ascended Masters, all for the highest expression on all levels.

From the Cosmos and Universe, we learn of other steps along the way. Together, we release judgment and blame; yet we move ahead with discernment and compassion. We create the highest.

We unite in Christ Holy Spirit and with our Star brothers and sisters in Love and Light, honoring all Life!

We are free from struggle and aligned with higher Love.

Invocation to the Holy of Holies

We call to the Holy of Holies,
        Kadosh, Kadosh, Kadosh, Adonai,
        Adonai Sabaoth!
Holy, Holy, Holy, Lord God of Hosts
        Praise God heaven and earth
        Praise God most high!

        Amen, Amen, and Amen

- Hebrew Invocation to God (public domain)

Note: The Holy of Holies is the innermost part of the Jewish Tabernacle Sacred Temple where the Arc of the Covenant was kept in Jerusalem. (reference page 97)

The Sacred Medicine Wheel

I AM the Sacred Medicine Wheel,
living and breathing Love and Light!
I AM one with the greater God essence
that blesses us all,
that is the energetic core
of our being and all creation.
I honor the Four Sacred Elements and Seven Directions
that are our alignment with Spirit,
that energetically charge our lives,
and teach us about these aspects of empowerment
that are truly within ourselves
and connected with Spirit.

We are the living expression of all aspects of the medicine wheel. The teaching is not about how to handle energy to get what we want. It's about understanding that we *are* the Sacred Medicine Wheel, and it's about our relationship with Spirit and Nature.

We learn that Light flows between all dimensions of creation as well as within ourselves. It's about simple truth, the flow of Light to balance us within. It's also about our interactions with everything outside of us.

The Native Americans know us to be related to all of nature and all of creation. They experience this powerful connection energetically and know that we are all One. They feel this relationship with great passion and cannot understand those who do not feel this connection.

These are Sacred relationships that encompass all life and life in the hereafter. The Lakota use the expression "Mitakuye Oyasin" to mean "All our relations"—this includes all of life: Mother Earth, Father Sky, people, nature, animals, plants, the mineral kingdom, and the elements, plus our cosmic universe and beyond. God is within all this!

It is for us to realize and to know that we are in a loving environment and at one with a loving God whose energy flows through everything and everybody.

The Shaman knows that the natural order of things is for a loving God to want to nurture and support God's children. If we see this truth already in place where we were once seeing apparent discrepancy, we can be a catalyst for higher truth and harmony to come forward.

Our meditation then is to feel our Oneness with the love and support of Spirit and to know freedom. We also can meditate to get in touch with our personal truth on higher levels. As we ask for the highest and best and receive guidance, we know that we are getting the most loving direction for our lives.

We have freedom of choice to let go of bondage and to receive the most love and support possible, far beyond our imagination.

As we meditate with the Sacred Medicine Wheel to get in touch with nature and with truth, we inherently get more clarity, and the quiet power of the universe reveals tremendous nurturing and support for our expression.

Historically, the Sacred Medicine Wheel has been used by Native American cultures; however, it has also been used in one form or another by Eastern and Western cultures, Hebrew, Druid, and Wicca traditions, and numerous other magical traditions. Down through history, many cultures and traditions have used the medicine wheel as a very powerful means of anchoring Light and establishing a vortex of energy flowing from sky to earth and from earth returning back to sky. They live this truth.

These ceremonies are a part of everyday life for many peoples, and represent religious connection to God and to nature. This is a universal means of establishing a Sacred Space for prayer.

In addition to these histories, almost every Native American nationality has a legend about White Buffalo Calf Woman, and the stories are very similar.

As the legend goes, two Indian Bucks were out hunting when they came upon a beautiful maiden. One wanted to rush down and make love to her. The other was holding back. As they approached the maiden, White Buffalo Calf Woman said to wait, but the first Buck wanted to go ahead and make love. So, she said to come ahead.

As they embraced, they began to swirl around, moving forward in time as the first Buck turned to dust and bones. White Buffalo Calf Woman then told the second Buck to remember what had happened there and report back to the tribe.

She had come to bring the teaching of the Sacred Medicine Wheel as a way to connect to Great Spirit in prayer, and to understand that lusting after the physical world would not last. Only by connecting with higher levels of Spirit could they find love and peace, and everlasting life!

The great gift to them was the ceremonial pipe, symbolic of how to pray—the bowl of the pipe representing the feminine energy in Mother Earth, the stem representing the masculine, and the Four Directions representing the Four Sacred Elements, so the tribe would always remember to pray and to connect with higher truth.

In the Native American Tradition

ALL PARTICIPANTS enter the medicine wheel from the East and walk in a clockwise direction around the circle until reaching the place in which they feel drawn to stand for the ceremony. With all participants standing, the following invocations are to be spoken aloud by the Shaman or other leader of the group as the group is directed to face the different directions of the medicine wheel.

The group may choose to speak these aloud with the leader. This ceremony can be performed by an individual as well by simply replacing the word "We" with the word "I" . . .

Looking Inward

"We call ourselves to center in alignment with Spirit on all levels, and call ourselves to ground. We call the truth forward from the Great Mystery of our heart. We call to Mother Earth and ask Her to connect with us. We feel the nurturing and support flowing up from Mother Earth."

Looking Up

"We call to Father Sky and give thanks from our heart for Light to come down through us and return to Mother Earth."

Looking Down

"We call to Grandmother-Mother Earth and give thanks from our heart for Light to come up through us and return to Father Sky, creating a Sacred Space." (Grandmother is the perfect expression of Mother Earth throughout time.)

Facing East

"We give thanks for the Blessings that come in the name of Archangel Raphael, and we call forth the Sacred Element of Air, which is consciousness and new awareness, flashes of insight, as well as birth and rebirth. From our heart, we give thanks and we welcome you."

Facing South

"We give thanks for the Blessings in the name of Archangel Michael, and we call forth the Sacred Element of Fire, which is clearing and purification, and awakens the innocence of the child. From our heart, we give thanks and we welcome you."

Facing West

"We give thanks for the Blessings in the name of Archangel Gabriel, and we call forth the Sacred Element of Water, which is understanding and the flow of Spirit within ourselves and within the connective spiral that connects us to all of Love and Light and All That Is. From our heart, we give thanks and we welcome you."

Facing North

"We give thanks for the Blessings in the name of Archangel Uriel, and we call forth the Sacred Element of Earth, which is the practical expression of Spirit and practical wisdom. From our heart, we give thanks and we welcome you."

Facing East

"As we close this circle that joins us in this Sacred Space, Father Sky and Christ Holy Spirit above flow down through us, connecting with our heart and anchoring into Mother Earth below our feet. Light flows up from Mother Earth, connecting through our heart, and returns to Father Sky. This is our energetic, free flowing, vertical alignment with God that extends into all dimensions. As we look to feel these energies, they come alive! In this Sacred Space, we anchor all these energies and more in consciousness for humanity and Mother Earth, establishing a vortex in the center of the medicine wheel as an entrance into the womb of Mother Earth Herself."

Facing the Center of the Medicine Wheel

"We now call to God the Highest with the Hermes levels of the Universe, the Ancient Hebrew levels of creating on each Tree of Life, Christ Holy Spirit, the 104 Sacred Lakota Energies, Divine Father and Mother God energies, the Seven Rays and corresponding Archangels, the Sacred Flames, and Ascended Masters, along with the Great Brotherhood of Light!

"We call forth these Great Bodies of Light to anchor through our center; that is, to visualize and see Light streaming from above and through our hearts, connecting to Mother Earth as we feel this steady flow of Love, compassion, understanding, harmony, peace, and joy."

These words bring tears to the eyes of the Shaman for they know the magnitude of Love and Light that they are tapping into; however, it is the experience that gives these words meaning. Those who are ahead on their path introduce us to this experience. We in turn become activated and go on to teach others. Once we have experienced this love connection, the words and symbolism take on tremendous meaning.

We commit ourselves to this great movement of expansion and the raising of consciousness for ourselves, for humanity, for Mother Earth and beyond!

All the gifts of Father and Mother God shall naturally flow to us as we are supported and blessed! As we know this as truth, we then see confirmation in our lives!

Aho

Medicine Wheel
Vortex

Father Sky

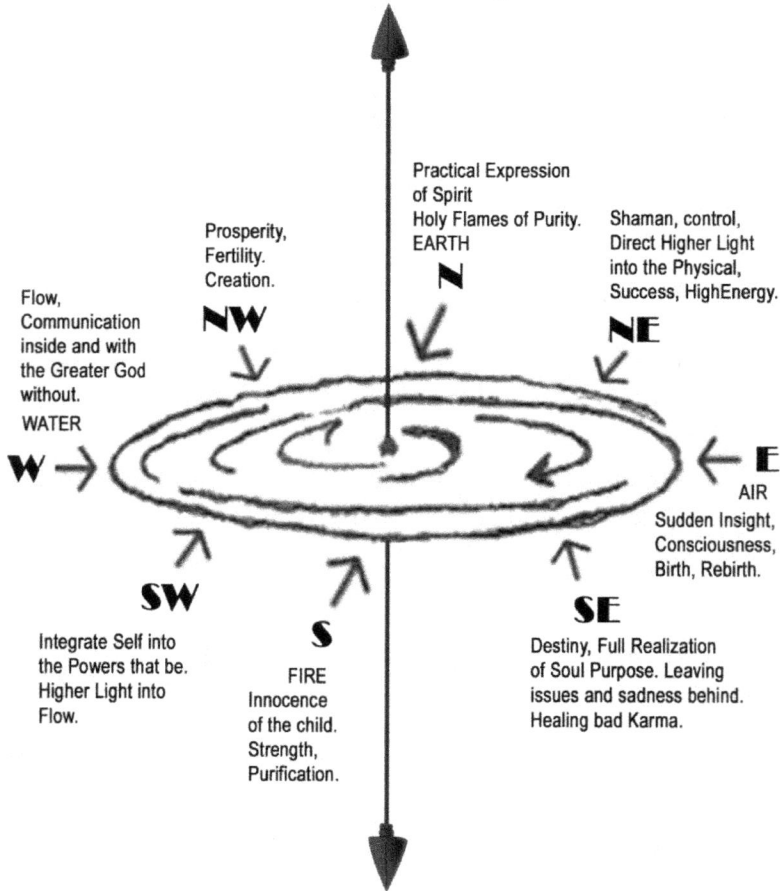

Prosperity,
Fertility.
Creation.

NW

Flow,
Communication
inside and with
the Greater God
without.

WATER

W

Practical Expression
of Spirit
Holy Flames of Purity.
EARTH

N

Shaman, control,
Direct Higher Light
into the Physical,
Success, HighEnergy.

NE

E

AIR
Sudden Insight,
Consciousness,
Birth, Rebirth.

SW

S

SE

Integrate Self into
the Powers that be.
Higher Light into
Flow.

FIRE
Innocence
of the child.
Strength,
Purification.

Destiny, Full Realization
of Soul Purpose. Leaving
issues and sadness behind.
Healing bad Karma.

Mother Earth

Contemplate the New Year

Here we are again at the beginning of another new year. Business is constantly changing. Our personal lives have new dramas and adventures. This is a take-off on the familiar "making of new year's resolutions."

Michael and Dianna are friends of mine who live in Saint Augustine, Florida. They recommend a simple process for clearing old issues and putting new intentions out to the universe for the New Year.

First, we take time to meditate and take inventory of all the things we have experienced during the past year. We look at the struggles and successes, looking also for a higher theme or pattern of flow in our lives. We might see a direction of growth and understanding in our experiences.

With this overview, we can ask for guidance and direction for the New Year and make this our intention. I strongly recommend that we all take time at the changing of the year for this process of releasing the old and welcoming the new. It is well worth the effort.

God Bless and Happy New Year!

Earth Acupuncture Meditation

The Three-Breath Sequence
to Activate and Direct a Life-Energy Beam[8]

This meditation technique may, with practice, be done anywhere at any time. It is best for both you and the earth to do the meditation in a quiet place when you have no need to rush away. Indoors is fine; outside, sitting directly on the earth is best. The technique is very simple. Sit with your eyes closed and begin to gently control your breath so that each breath is long and slow, and soft, and the inhalation and exhalation are of equal duration. Breathe slowly enough so that you are able to really feel each part of each breath. It is important to understand that the slowing down of your breath serves to focus your attention so that you can begin to feel the celestial and terrestrial energies entering into and passing through your body. These energies do not come into body through the breath; rather they pass through the top of your head and base of your spine. Breathing in a slow, regular manner allows you to feel these energies, add your own energy of love to them, and then direct this combined energy outward from your body as a life-energy beam. Do the three-breath sequence at least ten times whenever you sit to practice. If you have more time and want to have an intimate relationship with these energies, practice the sequence for thirty minutes to an hour every day. In the first few weeks or months of practicing this meditation, it may be necessary for you to mentally visualize the celestial and terrestrial energies passing through your body. With consistent practice, you will begin physically to feel the energies, and then you will realize that they are in fact always flowing through your Being. The more you practice this technique, the deeper will you experience connection to and love for the living earth.

BREATH # 1
CELESTIAL ENERGY

DURING INHALATION: Bring celestial energies into your heart. Energies enter the body through the crown chakra at the top of the head and come down to the heart chakra.

DURING EXHALATION: Add your own energy of consciousness and then direct both energies down through the root chakra, at the base of the spine, into the earth.

BREATH #2
TERRESTRIAL ENERGY

DURING INHALATION: Bring terrestrial energies into your root chakra, at the base of the spine, and up to the heart chakra.

DURING EXHALATION: Add your own energy of consciousness, and then direct both energies up through the crown chakra, at the top of the head, to the celestial realm.

BREATH #3
BOTH ENERGIES
(AT THE SAME TIME)

DURING INHALATION: Bring both celestial and terrestrial energies into your heart at the same time.

DURING EXHALATION: Add your own energy of consciousness to celestial and terrestrial energies; send all three energies out from your heart every direction, as in a constantly expanding Sphere. After the exhalation, begin with breath #1 again.

[8]Permission to reprint from Sacred Mountain Pilgrimages - Martin Gray - www.sacredsites.com

We meditate to listen
We pray to give thanks
We invoke the Light to empower
We chant to celebrate

- John Pollock

VII
UNDERSTANDING KARMA
AND POTENTIAL

This chapter goes into the reasons for karma: how to understand it, steps to take in minimizing its disruptive effects, as well as how to help others along with ourselves to accept positive life-affirming experiences.

With free choice also comes the process of manifesting through the laws of Man. These laws of Man are based on "justice"—in contrast to the grace and gentleness that comes with the laws of God operating through pure Love.

Briefly, the law of karma is also the law of "cause and effect." Our human feelings, thoughts, and actions set energies into motion that return to us. In layman's terms, "what goes around comes around."

The Karmic Board may be viewed as a panel of Light Beings whose job it is to help make sure karma is balanced in the physical world and on all other levels as well.

There are three ways to balance karma. The first is "retribution"—repaying what is owed, so to speak, to whom it is owed. The second is "atonement"—doing lots of good deeds to balance out past recriminations. The third is transformation through the Grace of God.

Transformation through the Grace of God involves intent to lift others along with ourselves through our opening to receive more light flowing in our lives. This also involves experiencing more joy and fulfillment, and more blessings for all of life. This may be the most pleasant way to balance karma—working through dispensation, grace, and forgiveness of ourselves, thereby opening the doors to forgiveness of others and by others. We simply ask for help to release what we're creating and bless the creation of something new.

Perhaps the most important realization for me was the insight that God has only the bright essence of God from which to create humankind and the worlds of nature.

We all have empowerment and connection with the essence of God flowing through us, whether we choose to act with Spirit or as an individual acting on our own, exercising our own free will. We may choose to experience a life of fulfillment or a life of lack and abandonment— either choice is empowered by our very essence of God within us and by what we want to experience.

Upon creating humankind with free will to express and to experience, it was also necessary to create a means of balancing the responsibility for all that was created. If heaviness is allowed to build up completely unchecked, it could only lead to destruction of our beautiful planet.

What I've seen is that we are all responsible for our own creations. As an extension of God, we all carry the unlimited potential to transmute, transform, and recreate our own reality, as well as contribute to a change in mass consciousness.

The Karmic Board is here to help all of us balance our creations, as well as our contractual agreements with others, in order to maintain the fragile balance of heaviness on earth with Love and Light of a higher vibration! This allows humankind to continue in this place of higher learning called life!

VIII

OVERVIEW OF THE SACRED ENERGIES AND LIGHT BEINGS

The Sanctuary of Light once located in the Black Forest near Colorado Springs, had a sign posted on the premises with a great quotation from the Eastern prophet, Khalil Gibran. It read, "Heaven has many doorways so that all who seek truth may enter!"

The purpose for working with many Beings of Light is for greater empowerment of our truth, greater healing, and a deeper understanding of our relationship with God. Whatever we learn about God, there is always a still greater expression to surprise us. As we grow, the nature of God seems to grow both ahead of us and with us; and we are a part of it.

As we expand in experience and service, we find that the true miracles take place when we are holding a sacred space for prayer and leaving the outcome to Spirit!

Light provides higher consciousness, purification, higher insights, better choices, and greater possibilities. With ever-expanding consciousness, we have greater awareness, the gift of discernment to get past our own judgments, and the opportunity to lift our ever-changing realities. We've become accustomed to living with certain issues that are our own. When exposed to more Light, these issues are charged and come forward to be understood, experienced, and released to spirit. Our energy field becomes lighter and we take another step in our process of enlightenment.

This chapter contains a basic description of some of the major energies that we invoke in this book. This helps us to connect with different Light consciousness and raise our vibration. There is much more to learn about working with these energies, but this chapter introduces some of the energies that I have found most valuable. These help us to align on higher levels of Light and contribute to our own great spiritual adventure!

I share my experiences here in prayer that they will prove to be a catalyst to reach the right people at the right time!

Hermes Thrice-Great Trismegistus
And Gnosis of Spirit

History and legend have come together to reveal one of the most incredible and far-reaching stories to affect humankind. In Greek, the word "Hermes" means "Messenger of the Gods." Hermes deals with wisdom, knowledge, and self-realization. Hermes, being widely thought of by the Greeks as a parallel to the Titan Prometheus, brought the element of fire to the earth-plane.

Hermes Trismegistus signed his name as the author of the Emerald Tablet—an ancient tablet made of emerald or similar emerald green crystalline substance, thought to be much older than 3000 B.C. and inscribed with Phoenician lettering. This tablet was thought to be rediscovered in the tomb of Hermes by Alexander the Great in 332 B.C. Its present location is debated among many archeologists, historians, and scholars.

Hermes' doctrine in the Emerald Tablet states that all things are an adaptation or an extension of the "One Thing" which is God. Hermes deals with the hidden energies and consciousness that are behind soul, spirit, and the mysteries of matter. The concept of all creation as an extension of one God can be seen at the foundations of many religions and philosophies from antiquity. As we learn of each new form of expression for Hermes, our personal awareness and understanding expands.

It would seem from the many and varied accounts in history that Hermes has expressed himself through whatever incarnation and whatever form necessary to expand our understanding of the universe. This expansion always involves our own personal relationship with God, and sheds light on a vast universe that is far beyond human comprehension. It involves initiation and movement to higher levels of understanding and consciousness. Hermes is with us in our dreams. He is the "Revealer of the Hidden" and "Lord of Rebirth." He is higher mind and inner knowledge. He provides guidance into alternate states of consciousness and enlightenment for humankind and provides a way for us to become integrated with God. As our guide to alternate levels of consciousness, he embodies the rational powers of the Sun (masculine nature) as well as the intuitive, irrational powers of the Moon (feminine nature) and our unseen connection to Spirit (Soul).

In three specific lives, Hermes Thrice-Great Trismegistus was considered to be an aspect of God who appeared in Light Body form and physical embodiment, each time reconnecting with his life's work from a previous life and furthering his contributions to our discovery of the nature of man and the structure of the universe.

The first of these three lives was his incarnation as "Thoth"—sometimes referred to as Thoth the Atlantean. Records as far back as the pre-Dynastic period tell us the Egyptians knew him as their God of all learning and hidden knowledge. He was said to be responsible for teaching men how to interpret things, arrange logical patterns of speech, and write down their thoughts. He was the inventor of Egyptian hieroglyphics and recordkeeping. He founded the sciences of mathematics, astronomy, and medicine. He represented the archetype of the "Word of God" or "Source of The Word." As Thoth, he is without any predecessor or parents. The power of

His Will emanates through his words and then comes to pass. What he says manifests—he literally speaks it into existence.

Hermes Thoth is the "recorder and balancer" and oversees the "weighing of the heart" ceremony to determine who will enter heaven. He also wrote in a scroll called "The Book of Breathings" which explains how humans become Gods through alchemy of the spirit.

As the archetype of Hermes above, Thoth had allegedly hidden the sum of all knowledge and the Emerald Tablet inside two pillars for safety before the Great Flood. One of these pillars was at Heliopolis and the other at Thebes. The pillars were said to be protected so they could only be accessed by those who would be sure to oversee and protect this great knowledge for humanity.

According to Dr. Livingston, a well-known scholar, the Great Flood most likely took place somewhere around the year 3000 B.C. There are accounts of this flood from many sources including Eastern Scripture and the Bible. This lifetime of Thoth has been documented as far back as records can go, and stems from antiquity.

Jewish mystics identify Thoth with Seth, the second son of Adam from the Bible. They credit Seth as writing the Emerald Tablet and hiding it in a cave near Hebron to later be discovered by Sarah, the wife of Abraham. The Torah mentions seven universal laws to be given to humankind, very much like the Emerald Tablet.

Thoth is also associated with Idris of the Koran. Idris was also associated with Enoch by the Hebrews in the Jewish Old Testament. "Enoch" means the "Initiated One" and is portrayed in Genesis as an angelic being who could travel through dimensional realms much like our accounts of Hermes and

Hermes as Thoth. Enoch is also identified with Metatron who deals with the structure of the universe. The Sepher Yezirah, one of the most famous of the ancient Qabalistic texts, tells us that all of creation emanates from the thoughts of the One Mind—much like the teachings of the Emerald Tablet and the symbolism that is used in initiations by the Order of the Golden Dawn, a system known as Enochian Magic.

The second main life of Hermes was that of an Egyptian pharaoh born as Amenhotep IV, meaning "Amen is Satisfied." Amenhotep IV lived after the Great Flood. His reign lasted about 17 years—1351 B.C. to 1334 B.C. "Amen" was celebrated as God, as it was in Amen Ra (God as chief or king of all gods), as it is also at the end of modern prayers today . . . Amen.

There are many interesting facts about Amenhotep IV's life. After he came to power, he changed the Egyptian religious structure from the worship of many gods to the worship of the One Thing he called the Sun God ("the disk"). Amenhotep IV taught that the One Thing was formless and subtle until we put thought to the Rays, which then gave it form and shape.

Amenhotep IV changed his name to Akhenaten as he came to celebrate the One God "Aten." Amen (Ammon or Amoun) was considered the Chief deity among many of Egypt, Lord of all, the God who engendered himself and the rest of the gods. Amen was also represented as Amen Ra. Aten (Aton) was the God imagined by the first monotheist Akhenaten, who envisioned his One God as the disk of the sun. Aten was declared by Akhenaten to be the only God, not just the Chief god. Akhenaten declared all other gods of Egypt to be non-existent. Because of this, Akhenaten was called the Heretic Pharaoh, making a complete break with tradition to worship only the One God—the spiritual difference between the worship of Amen and the worship of Aten being the difference between polytheism and monotheism.

Akhenaten was androgynous in appearance. Statues show him with an elongated head and fine facial features. He had drooping shoulders and a pear-shaped body with thin, weak legs. He has been called the "Extraterrestrial King" for his appearance. He had two co-rulers, both called "Beauty of all Beauties"—Nefertiti and Smenkhkare. It is hypothesized that Akhenaten may have rediscovered information from Hermes Tristmegistus and the Emerald Tablet to enable him to complete the pyramid of Cheops.

Akhenaten introduced the new concept of "living in truth" and integrating principles of The One. Both he and Nefertiti suddenly disappeared at the end of his reign. This led to a lot of speculation as to what happened prior to his disappearance, and the idea that he may have come to a violent death. Today, through DNA testing, archeologists believe they have confirmed the find of his mummy and several relatives. There is much more investigating to be done.

After Akhenaten disappeared, he was replaced by his ten-year-old son, Tutankhaten. Tutankhaten's name was soon after changed to Tutankhamun or Tutankhamen (servant of

Amen). This was the start of the reign of the boy-king, "King Tut." King Tut reinstated the old religions and attempted to remove all signs of monotheism. Even though Egypt's religion was returned to polytheism, the effects of Akhenaten's prior focus on the One God would affect all religions from that time forward.

After conquering Egypt in 331 B.C., Alexander the Great crossed the desert to an ancient Libyan temple in Siwa near the tomb of Hermes. Alexander felt he was destined to reveal the ancient secrets to the world, so he took the Emerald Tablet and other Hermes scrolls from the tomb to Heliopolis. He placed the Emerald Tablet on public display before hiding it once again, possibly having returned it to the tomb of Hermes. The original Emerald Tablet was written with the Phoenician alphabet, and Alexander had his scribes translate it into Greek and hieroglyphics. Copies of the Emerald Tablet then traveled through Arabia and on to Spain and Europe despite the later burnings of the libraries at Alexandria.

The third great life of Hermes Thrice-Great Trismegistus was a young man named Balinas. An attempt to determine the timeline of Balinas would have him living around 64 B.C. Balinas had meditated at the tomb of Hermes Thrice-Great since the age of fourteen. The tomb was located just outside the town of Tyana in what is now known as Turkey. At sixteen, Balinas read the inscriptions on the tomb once again and took the messages literally.

One message said "Behold! I am Hermes Trismegistus, he who is threefold in wisdom . . ." The other said, "Let him who would learn and know the secrets of creation and nature, inquire beneath my feet." Taking this message literally, Balinas dug at the site. It is said that he found a cavern with the mummified remains of Hermes and four books with original writings from Hermes. Also, in the mummy's hand was the Emerald Tablet. Balinas then traveled and taught the meditation process and initiations of Hermes Thrice-Great. He traveled through Spain and Europe and beyond to India, sharing Hermes' teachings and healing. His closest friends knew that Balinas would bi-locate himself from time to time. Balinas spent the rest of his life in enlightenment and at one with the "One Thing" in meditation.

The differing accounts would suggest that there were more than one Hermes. Much earlier Greek Hermes was the same as the Roman God Mercury. He was best known as the messenger of the Gods through Greek Mythology. Enoch has the same qualities as Hermes Thrice-Great moving from one dimension to another. He may have been the same Being. Many Hindus believe Hermes was Buddha. Concepts are similar to Taoism, Hinduism, and Buddhism, as well as Judaism, Christianity, and Islam. Hermes Thrice-Great may very well have threads of existence in many more places than we have realized in the past.

The pyramids are now believed to be over ten thousand years old, and the Emerald Tablet may go back as far as ten thousand years or more. Hermes Trismegistus identifies himself as the author of the Emerald Tablet. There is no accurate way to gauge the lives of Gods that lived in antiquity before the legends of Hermes Thrice-Great Tristmegistus of Egypt.

In the Greek play Ion, Euripides had Hermes introduce himself in the following way:

"Atlas, who wears on back of bronze a symbol, the ancient Abode of the Gods in heaven, had a daughter whose name was Maia, born of a goddess: She lay with Zeus, and bore me, Hermes, servant of the immortals."

From Greek mythology, we see that Hermes' grandfather is Atlas, who is part mortal and part immortal. He holds up heaven. Maia was his mother, and she had a goddess as her mother. This would make Zeus Hermes' father. Zeus is known as one of the highest of Gods. The lineage was poised to give inspiration to Hermes that he then built upon and brought forward as consciousness and higher understanding.

The ancient Rosetta Stone was text written on a rock slab dating back to 196 B.C. It was a decree issued by King Ptolemy V in Memphis, Egypt. Fragments have been found dating back to 238 B.C. that were part of the same decree, the Decree of Canopus. The Rosetta Stone contains three scripts of the same document, the Emerald Tablet. This supports the legends of Thrice-Great Hermes of antiquity. It was able to give scholars a chance to compare ancient Egyptian hieroglyphics, ancient Greek, and Egyptian Demotic script, which was expanded with ancient Greek. The earlier language of hieroglyphics had ceased to be used. Having three different versions of the same text enabled historians to begin to understand hieroglyphics and make future translations possible.

The Emerald Tablet

B. J. Dobbs found the following translation in the alchemical papers by Sir Isaac Newton:

1. 'Tis true without lying, certain most true.

2. That which is below is like that which is above that which is above is like that which is below to do the miracles of one only thing.

3. And as all things have been arose from one by the mediation of one: so all things have their birth from this one thing by adaptation.

4. The Sun is its father, the moon its mother,

5. the wind hath carried it in its belly, the earth its nurse.

6. The father of all perfection in the whole world is here.

7. Its force or power is entire if it be converted into earth.

7a. Separate thou the earth from the fire, the subtle from the gross sweetly with great industry.

8. It ascends from the earth to the heaven again it descends to the earth and receives the force of things superior and inferior.

9. By this means ye shall have the glory of the whole world thereby all obscurity shall fly from you.

10. Its force is above all force. for it vanquishes every subtle thing and penetrates every solid thing.

11a. So was the world created.

12. From this are and do come admirable adaptations whereof the means (Or process) is here in this.

13. Hence I am called Hermes Trismegist, having the three parts of the philosophy of the whole world.

14. That which I have said of the operation of the Sun is accomplished and ended.

Hermes Trismegistus stated on his tomb, "Behold! I am Hermes Trismegistus, he who is threefold in wisdom." He represents to us the three parts of the philosophy of the whole world. The first is "SPIRIT," the Sun (our rational, masculine nature). The Second is "CONSCIOUSNESS," which is Soul (our unseen connection to God). The third is "FORM," the Moon (our irrational, intuitive, and feminine nature). Everything is made up of energy. Seeing how Spirit, Consciousness, and Form play out in our world gives us insight to all creation. These three energies make up the understanding of the whole world. Masculine, Feminine, and Soul infuses life into worldly creation, and opens us to higher dimensions of Divine Mind.

In addition, the famous quote "As above, so below" comes from the Emerald Tablet. It involves the understanding that there is only One God that is the Mind of God that is Above. There is also only One Thing that is Below which encompasses the material world and all the planets. As Above, so Below. This understanding is critical in the processes of alchemical operations in the evolution of the soul and enlightenment.

Dennis William Hauck was asked in channeling meditation if these terms correspond to our concepts of heaven above and hell below. Hermes reply was:

"Such labels are inventions that serve worldly ends, for the true Above and Below are living things beyond description. In my tablet, I have revealed all that can be spoken of these unlimited regions. The Above is the abode of the One Mind, and the Below is the abode of the One Thing. You need know nothing more because nothing more is knowable; you cannot label the ineffable. Work instead with the tiny spark of consciousness of which you are possessed; that spark can be fanned into a blazing gnosis that burns away the falsity of your tragic self-deception. Thereafter can you verify for yourself that of which I speak. You can behold the One Mind; you can touch the One Thing . . . Listen carefully. Thought is a bubble of being that erupts on the fabric of reality through the Pattern I revealed in my tablet. Thus, you are as mortal as your thoughts, and it is your notion of heaven and hell that keeps you earthbound because it weighs you down with fear and duplicity. The things whereof I speak are everywhere under your nose; you have only to reach out to touch them. But out of your arrogance have you denied the One Mind, and out of your fear have you desecrated the One Thing.

"*The only hope for mankind is the alchemy revealed in my living tablet. But be not mistaken; the alchemy of which I speak is working with your seeming valueless thoughts and feelings to refine them to operate on all levels with the same force with which they work in Divine Mind. In truth, all that you are and all I am is thoughts and feelings, yet all thoughts are just from One Mind and all feelings are in just One Thing. Therefore, your consciousness is both a part and the whole. Know that the One Thing within you is your chaotic feelings, rejected energy that can drive your transformation . . . . Know that the union of thought and feeling is like a stone you can carry anywhere, for this intelligence of the heart is everywhere just One Thing.*"[9]

One main realization from the Emerald Tablet is that the creative energies of the One Thing are subtle and permeate all dense matter. By sympathy and feeling physical matter, we can raise ourselves to very high and rarified levels of "The One" by using our right and true imagination. We can then feel the high creative energies that everything has come from and imagine bringing those back down with us. The creative energies have no form until our mind becomes one with the "One Thing" on a spiritual axis. Then suddenly, we are one with the "One Thing" on the highest levels for healing and transformation. This is the basis for personal alchemy in our lives.

Mind reveals to Hermes in the Corpus Hermeticum and Hermetic Tradition XI of the Gnostic Society Library that the structure of creation has levels within levels as vibrations and consciousness that are stepped down to create our material world. Although each level has a different function, the descent of Light is not linear. The energies are multi-dimensional. The energies of Divine Mind are constantly in motion. They are under constant pressure to fill all levels of consciousness within, and to fill all souls with Light. All things that are alive have a soul and sustain life at their particular level. The Light is constantly swirling to lower dimensions and back up to higher dimensions.

We call ourselves into alignment with the Hermes descending levels of creation. God is everywhere and is our Highest Source. Highest Source contains the level of Aeon within which is lastingness and deathlessness. Aeon contains the level of Cosmos within which is restoration and opposites. Cosmos contains the level of Time within which is change—increase and decrease. Time has the level of Genesis within which is life and death. Our Universe contains our Planetary System with all the energies for life within. We feel and sense our connection with the Highest and move back down, returning to earth level. We give thanks for our alignment and the blessings on all levels! We pray that we are elevated and supported in our highest service and in our highest expression.

[9]*The Emerald Tablet*, Printed by Penguin/Arkana.
Copyright Dennis William Hauk, 1999 quote by permission.

Historical reference:
Thrice Greatest Hermes, a trilogy written by G.R.S. Mead, Mind unto Hermes structure of creation.

The Ancient Hebrew Tree of Life

This ancient wisdom was given to the Hebrews by God. It is the diagram of how to create or manifest. On the surface, it appears to be totally mental in structure, but this information is a foundation upon which to create and manifest in the physical world.

The Tree of Life consists of ten positions (plus one other not often used). These positions are each referred to as a "sephira" located on the Tree of Life. Each sephira represents a different meaning and sphere of influence of the powerful energies that are flowing through it. Included is a diagram of the Tree of Life naming each sephira. Each sephira has different attributes. The following gives the position of each sephira and its energetic meaning with corresponding Archangel and planetary influences.

The Hebrews describe the nature of God as Ain Soph Aur. This is "Limitless or Eternal Light." Every point within is the center. From this point of Light that is God, the Light begins its descent in the process of creating.

Kether

This "Light" steps down in vibration rate from Ain Soph Aur to the 1st sephira which is called "Kether." This is **1st Cause**. What is meant is that the first spark of idea or conception of what is to be created begins at this high level in Kether. Of the Higher Order of Beings, the mighty Metatron is at this level overseeing the structure and components of the universe.

The message that I received from Spirit was that Metatron, at the top of the Tree of Life, is the expansion of consciousness that is Transformation—different from the subsequent Rays of the Archangels—and is concerned with the *balancing* of the Silver Ray (the will of man on a spiritual level) with the Gold Ray (the will of God). These Rays each have a definite feel to them as well as definite purpose and definite characteristics. The meaning of "Kether" relates to origin of creating and is the number One (1) on the Tree of Life.

Chokhmah

The Light then steps down to the 2nd sephira called "Chokhmah" at the top of the right pillar. The Light at this level represents the number Two (2) on the Tree of Life. This sephira represents the concept of mirrors. This is a high level of force or dynamic action. The Archangel Ratziel is the same as Divine Father, and holds the Chokhmah path of consciousness and initiation. The entire right pillar represents masculine energy and displays Mercy.

Binah

From there the Light crosses over to the 3rd sephira called "Binah" at the top of the left pillar. The Light at this level represents the number Three (3) on the Tree of Life. This sephira represents form and deals with understanding and being receptive. The Archangel Tzaphiel is the same as Divine Mother, and holds the Binah path of consciousness and initiation. The entire left pillar represents feminine energy and displays Severity.

This is the Great Sea of Form. To relate this energetic connection to our own lives we might imagine things happening to us in terms of "1st Cause" (idea) plus "Force" (action) to carry out our plan and the form in which our plan is to take shape. As we continue with the path of descent, it is helpful to view these different levels from the function that each sephira serves.

Chesed

The Light then travels back again to the right pillar to the 4th sephira called "Chesed." Here, the Light is concerned with building up forces, adding on or expanding. This sephira also includes mercy and compassion. The Light at this level represents the number Four (4) on the Tree of Life, and can be imagined as the four corners of higher foundation. This could be buying a bigger house or hiring more employees in our business. The Archangel Tzadkiel is up-building and support, and holds the Chesed path of consciousness and initiation. This is the same Tzadkiel that serves us along with St. Germain and the Violet Transmuting Flame.

Geburah

The Light then steps down and crosses over to the left pillar to the 5th sephira called "Geburah" The Light at this level represents the number Five (5) on the Tree of Life. The energies here are breaking-down forces. This means severity or tempering with justice. Some examples might be spring-cleaning before summer, clearing out closets to make room for new fashions, or release of outdated mental patterns or emotions that no longer serve us. The Archangel Khamael holds the Geburah path of consciousness and initiation.

Tiphareth

The next step is down and to the center pillar to the 6th sephira called "Tiphareth." The Light at this level represents the number Six (6) on the Tree of Life. This level represents balance, beauty, and the "Bringers of Light." It is peace and harmony as well. Archangel Michael serves here with Christ and Buddha. The whole center pillar is balance between the left and right pillars and displays Mildness or Consciousness and Christ initiation.

Netzach

The next step goes down and over to the right pillar to the 7th sephira called "Netzach." The Light at this level represents the number Seven (7) on the Tree of Life. Netzach is victory over emotions. This is in regard to feeling emotions in order to let them flow through, yet returning to the higher understandings of life. This is about releasing and shifting to focus beyond past challenges. The Archangel Haniel holds the Netzach path of consciousness and initiation.

Hod

From here, the next step down is back to the left column to the 8th sephira called "Hod." The Light at this level represents the number Eight (8) on the Tree of Life. This is glory of the intellect. This involves getting free of the mind-traps of lower personality and rising into higher truth and reason of Spirit. It also involves spiritual ceremony that brings higher communication with Spirit. The Archangel Raphael holds the Hod path of consciousness and initiation.

Yesod

The next step takes us down and over to the center pillar to the 9th sephira called "Yesod." The Light at this level represents the number Nine (9) on the Tree of Life. This is what we refer to as the "astral plane." All thoughts reside here prior to coming into physical form. They are the foundations for physical reality. Although all thoughts and intentions go into the astral to create from an etheric level, not all thoughts are brought through into the physical reality. Some thoughts are not clearly expressed or not expressed with sufficient force to manifest; or other thoughts may interfere with them, creating a cancellation effect. Expressing a clear intention to the universe with great desire or passion along with a quick release works the best. The Archangel Gabriel holds the Yesod path of consciousness and initiation.

Malkuth

From Yesod we travel in a straight path down into the 10th sephira called "Malkuth." The Light at this level represents the number Ten (10) on the Tree of Life. Malkuth represents earth or physical level manifestation and completion. This level of Light contains the four elements of Air, Fire, Water, and Earth. We might think of this as "real" or worldly manifestation, even though from a spiritual perspective we might see this as the "illusion." The Archangel Sandalphon holds the Malkuth path of consciousness and initiation.

On the Tree of Life, the left pillar is feminine (form and severity), while the right pillar is masculine (force and mercy). The center pillar is balance (consciousness and mildness). Any work with the energy of a sephira on the right pillar should include work with its direct counterpart on the left pillar, and vice versa, to maintain balance. (For example, when working with Chokhmah on the right pillar, also work with Binah on the left pillar, etc.)

The path of descending Light is in the shape of a lightning bolt connecting the sephirot (plural) in a zigzag pattern, one to another, and descending to the level of earth. The spiritual roots of the "Tree" are in heaven and shine Light into Creation on earth.

Shown below is a diagram of the Tree of Life:

This single-tree diagram shows each sephira with its corresponding energies and purpose.

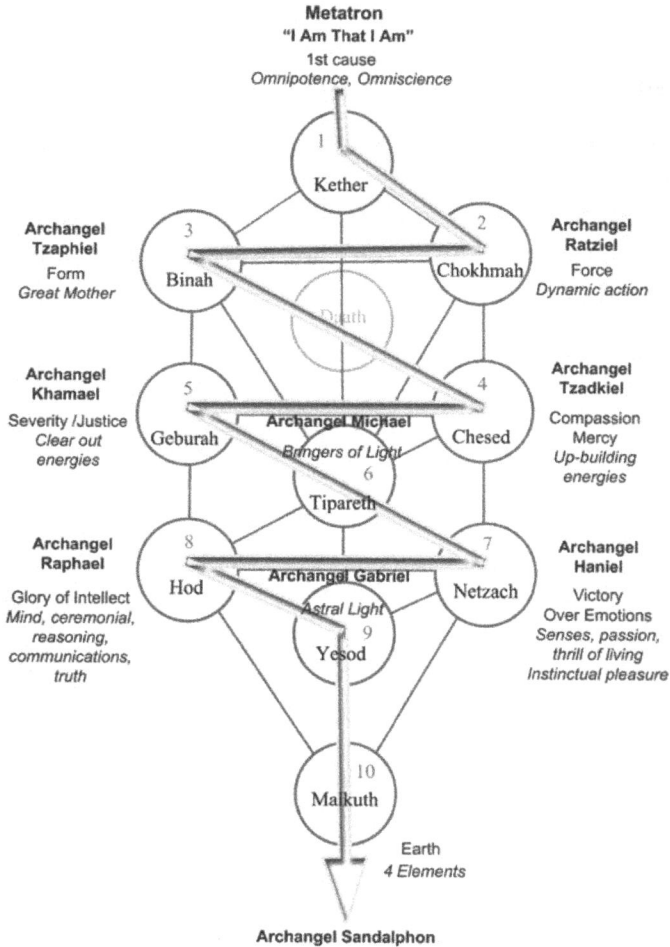

Metatron
"I Am That I Am"
1st cause
Omnipotence, Omniscience

1
Kether

Archangel
Tzaphiel

Form
Great Mother

3
Binah

2
Chokhmah

Archangel
Ratziel

Force
Dynamic action

Death

Archangel
Khamael

Severity /Justice
Clear out
energies

5
Geburah

Archangel Michael

Bringers of Light

6
Tipareth

4
Chesed

Archangel
Tzadkiel

Compassion
Mercy
Up-building
energies

Archangel
Raphael

Glory of Intellect
Mind, ceremonial,
reasoning,
communications,
truth

8
Hod

Archangel Gabriel

Astral Light

9
Yesod

7
Netzach

Archangel
Haniel

Victory
Over Emotions
Senses, passion,
thrill of living
Instinctual pleasure

10
Malkuth

Earth
4 Elements

Archangel Sandalphon

Next is the realization that there are four different levels or "worlds," each containing a total version of the Tree of Life. On each of these four worlds or levels, the bottom of one tree is the top of the next tree down as the energies continue to step down in vibration rate.

The path of descending Light in the shape of a lightning bolt moves through each sephira of the "Tree" and through all four "worlds" on the way to creating.

The Qabalah Cross is drawn in front of the body to symbolize the opening of each level of the Tree of Life. Begin with your hands in prayer position—palms together, fingers pointing upward. This is almost as if you hold the sword of Creation in your hands! With your hands in this position in front of your forehead, inhale deeply. With a powerful exhale, stroke down with intensity and intention. Immediately inhale deeply once again. And with a powerful exhale, stroke across left to right. Open the levels of Atziluth (emanation), Briah (creation), Yetzirah (formation), and Assiah (action).

Of the four "worlds," the first in its descent is the level of Atziluth or "Emanation" at the top. The next below is Briah or "Creation," then Yetzirah or "Formation," and finally Assiah or "Action" at the bottom of the creating process.

The "Qabalah Cross" is an invocation *motion*. We invoke the level of "Emanation" with the arms extended in front of the body, exhale swipe down, and exhale swipe across left to right at the heart center (in cross formation). Each cross symbolizes the invocation of all energies on the Tree of Life for each level or "world." Make a separate cross for each level—Emanation level, Creation level, Formation level, and Action level.

Please remember that when we activate these powerful energies, we need to be in balance, centered, and aware. We need to be ready and willing to do the work that will present itself in answer to this calling.

Shown below is a diagram of the Four Worlds Tree of Life:
This four-tree diagram illustrates a three dimensional view
of the four levels for creating.

The Four Worlds

"Emanation"
Atziluth

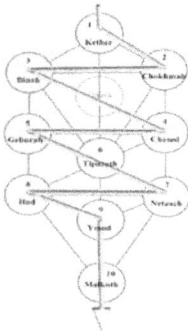

"Creation"
Briah

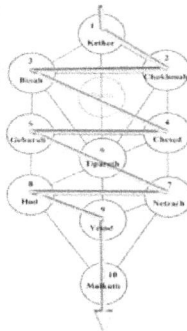

"Formation"
Yetzirah

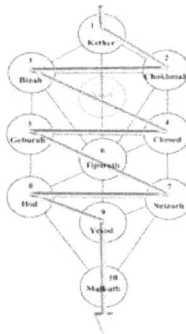

"Action"
Assiah

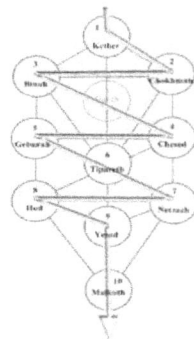

The final thing to know here is that we can invoke the energies of each level—feeling, visualizing, and breathing the descent of Light from heaven downwards and into our lives!

If we want to work on personal mastery, the paths between one sephira and another have personal lessons for each of us. The Tree of Life shows the paths between the sephirot being the same paths as the major Arcana in the tarot deck. Each major Arcana is an initiation of understanding and new level of awareness on our journey through the universe. We are each the "Fool" (the first card/step in the tarot's major Arcana) on our own path to experience the many lessons of the esoteric journey through the major Arcana, then stepping up to the knowledge and personal mastery of the "Magician." The "Magician" is both pure of heart and wise in the ways of the world. The entire esoteric journey leads to a full and rich understanding of the "World" (the final card/step in the tarot's major Arcana and esoteric journey). There is much more to learn here. I strongly recommend further study to discover deeper meanings of life.

Our purpose for now is to gain understanding of the energies of the Qabalah Tree of Life and to begin bringing those energies into our life so we can work with them for healing and manifesting.

An example of this might be bringing in the full gamut of energies on the levels of Emanation, Creation, Formation, and Action, and bringing the full scope of the creating process in for our highest purpose in our meditations.

Remember, when using the Qabalah Cross, swipe down our body and then swipe across with an inhale and exhale for each swipe and for each of the four levels. **Whoosh!** The energies move rapidly through the Tree of Life on all four levels and through us for the highest expression of Spirit and personal healing!

Some wonderful resources for more information about the Tree of Life, the Qabalah, and the Tarot are:

➢ *The Mystical Qabalah* by Dion Fortune
➢ *The Golden Dawn* by Israel Regardie
➢ Tree- Of-Life Tarot deck, Camphausen/Van Leeuwen, AGM Agmuller, ch-8212 Neushausen/Switzerland

Divine White Light
Used to Manifest our Ideal Life Vision[10]

Throughout history people have called on the energy of the Divine White Light to flow forth for protection, raising awareness, light, clarity, and transmutation of dense energies to release and transform. Meditations across the globe call in the White Light to flow into the crown and fill the entire aura. We are all able to access this energy for our use and guidance in the goals and spiritual intentions we have set for ourselves. The Divine Source is awaiting and aware of our connection at all times.

We tend to separate ourselves from awareness of the connection and the benefits of this connection during times of misalignment, stress, fear, and worry. At these times, we are seeing the world around us as well as ourselves from a filtered view, creating the illusion that the Divine does not see our situation or us. It is up to us to bring ourselves back into alignment with a clearer view of our Divine Source. The connection to Divine Source is always there for us to feel, but if we reside in lower frequencies we don't have awareness of it, therefore we are unable to have access to this infinite knowledge of Source, which we often call our intuition or our sixth sense. So in order to feel that connection we must raise our vibration to meet the vibration of the Divine. We can use the Divine White Light to do this.

Universal Law states that no Being can override the free will of another. That means we must ask for assistance and guidance. Even though Angels and Celestial Beings want to help us, they don't have permission unless we ask. We must want and ask for this Divine energy to flow forth toward us.

If we are seeking guidance, protection, clarity, or help transmuting old dense energies, we can ask that Divine White Light flow forth. The Celestial Beings and Divine Source cannot lower their vibration to come down to meet us; they can only shine brighter for us to see the light until we ask for help. We can bring this energy forth at any time. "Ask and ye shall receive." Simply set the intention. We call forth the Divine White Light to connect to our crown chakra and to flow through us, anchoring into Mother Earth.

We are learning how to create our lives with intention. We can combine the knowledge of the Law of Attraction with this Divine energy to speed up achievement of our goals. We can use the Divine White Light to transmute old dense vibrations from our energy field. We call on it, and the Divine White Light flows through and encompasses our whole Being, and releases any old dense energies—such as old thoughts or emotions that don't serve our highest good—into the earth to be recycled. As those energies release, it frees our energy field to rise to higher vibrations, and if we seek to deliberately connect to the Divine Source within this time, it trains our vibration to this higher frequency.

Holding ourselves in this high frequency vibration while deliberately bringing our thoughts to match the things we want in life and "feeling" our ideal life vision—these actions are the key to manifesting. Doing this often trains our vibration, carves out a familiar feeling place within us, and helps us align with this much more easily during daily life to bring us out of stressors. This is the power to create deliberate manifestation. We train ourselves into this alignment by holding that "feeling" as often as possible.

The key is to "feel" it as already "real" in the present moment. Once we seek the "feeling" of success, then the things that reflect success must come. We hold success as long as possible when we are in the feeling of it. We let the Divine White Light hold us in that feeling vibration as long as we can hold it. We bring ourselves back to that feeling as often as we can each day; this trains our vibration to it. Once we consistently vibrate it, the Law of Attraction must bring it to us. Of course, when we align with the Universe we still need to be honest with ourselves and align with our truth within.

[10]Reprinted by permission, Rheana Jackson, R.M.T.
www.GatekeeperHealing.com

The Energy of the Dove

When Lord Jesus Christ was baptized by John the Baptist, it was said that a dove appeared above His head. This was the grounding of the Holy Spirit to the earth. The energies of acceptance and forgiveness were among the beautiful gifts that Christ brought to humanity. These were gifts from His heart.

The energy of the Dove is the descent of the Holy Spirit through Christ flowing through us, then anchoring into Mother Earth. By visually seeing this in our mind's eye, we connect with this blessing and healing of our soul-spirit.

We also connect with the feeling of tremendous warmth and a melting of our heart with tremendous love and acceptance. We are forgiven so that we can therefore forgive ourselves. We can release the past and move forward without emotional baggage to continue influencing our lives. The effects are far-reaching.

We align ourselves with God on all levels through soul and higher self to the Highest.

We call ourselves to center, calling forth all the aspects of ourselves that resonate with Mother Earth. We call to Mother Earth and ask Her to connect with us in grounding, nurturing, and support. We see and feel the Holy Spirit coming through Christ and into our crown, through us, and into others for healing. The Light then returns to God through Mother Earth.

The forgiveness and acceptance has a tendency to bring about a healing experience that stays with us without reversal. The great Love brings to us quite a gift in understanding and healing, as well as changing our lives.

We see this and we feel this! We call to Lord Jesus Christ to surrender our will of personality and ego for higher purpose and for higher love. If we so choose, we may ask that He show us how this works in our lives; that He bend the aspects of our lives into alignment with the purpose of the Holy Spirit for healing.

By the Grace of God and Lord Jesus Christ,

Amen, Amen, and Amen, so be it

Note: This initiation took place for me in 1988, one year after the harmonic convergence. I had an experience of me asking guides what energies I should use for healing work with others and them telling me to use the energy of the Dove! It took me three weeks to find out what the energy of the Dove was. This whole experience was an eye-opening experience for me.

Reiki

Reiki is a spiritually-directed healing process where subtle universal life-force energy is drawn, not sent, through the hands to the perfect place in the body where it is needed. Reiki is a channeled energy that uses symbols on four Reiki levels to direct the energies into the body to physical, emotional, and mental levels. It is also used for long distance and spiritual healing through time and space.

Originally, Reiki was known as far back as the Ling Chi of the Chinese Taoists 5000 years ago. It was later found in the ancient sutras of India written in Sanskrit over 2500 years ago.

In the late 1800s, after being lost for several centuries, Reiki was rediscovered by a minister and ambassador for Japan named Mikao Usui. Mikao Usui had been searching for many, many years for the secret to Christ and Buddha healing. He studied the Christ teachings as well as other sacred teachings in Japan, China, India, and Tibet.

It all came to a head, so to speak, with a mystical experience in 1922 on the Holy Mountain of Kuriyama. It was reported that a huge ball of Light came out of the sky hitting Mikao Usui abruptly in the forehead area. He was blessed with an initiation and saw the symbols to provide the entire Reiki system. Reiki is a clear method of transfer of universal life-force from Spirit passed on through "attunement" initiations using Reiki symbols.

Reiki energy seems to be a combination of fire and water energies with the ability to seek out and go where it is needed. Once rediscovered, it was transferred to the mainland from Hawaii and continues to be taught in both eastern and western cultures today.

To use Reiki for healing, we visualize and call in all the Reiki symbols onto ourselves, on the chakras. We repeat each symbol's name aloud three times; taking three deep breaths with each, then exhale and visualize our alignment with God.

A wonderful resource for more information about Reiki - *Essential Reiki* by Diane Stein

霊
気

Johrei

Johrei is a spiritual healing process which is channeled much like Reiki. In Japanese "Johrei" means "purification of the spirit." It is a fire energy that brings Divine Light through to dissolve spiritual impurities that affect all levels of spirit, mind, body, and soul. Johrei is said to burn away the spiritual clouds and toxins that we have accumulated in life.

Mokichi Okada received the Divine Light through spiritual revelation in the year 1926. Johrei was then developed in Japan in the 1930s.

Mikao Usui who founded Reiki, was located nearby in Koyto, Japan, close to Mokichi Okada. Both Reiki and Johrei also receive empowerment through the Dai Ko Myo symbol.

Johrei uses an altar with calligraphy symbols on a paper scroll. The purpose is to promote peace, protection, balance, success, power, and righteousness. When working with Johrei, we pray for purification of the spiritual body in order to awaken our Divine spiritual nature. That brings manifesting and healing, the raising of vibrations, compassion, and the lifting of heaviness.

The prayers are for enlightenment, spiritual awakening, and inner peace, then physical and emotional healing follows. Avalokiteshvara is the celestial embodiment of compassion and enlightenment. He has given us the mantra, "Om Mani Padme Hum" which is perhaps the most repeated Buddhist chant. He is most highly regarded among Bodhisattvas returning to samsara (the cycle of death and rebirth to which life in the material world is bound).

To understand the magnitude of Avalokiteshvara we can look into the meaning of "Om Mani Padme Hum." This prayer has all the elements of the Buddhist teaching included in this one chant. The phrase literally means "Behold, the Jewel in the Lotus." This refers to our connection with the beautiful spirit of compassion and enlightenment that already resides within humankind. This state of compassion and enlightenment can be found within the lotus, which is the multifaceted link with God through the heart chakra, encompassing our own true nature.

Kalu Rinpoche, when speaking of Dharma, states that the six syllables of the mantra "Om Mani Padme Hum" have each a meaning:

OM

THE FIRST SYLLABLE "OM"
blesses us to achieve perfection in the practice of generosity.

MA

THE SECOND SYLLABLE "MA"
helps us to perfect the practice of pure ethics.

NI

THE THIRD SYLLABLE "NI"

helps us to achieve perfection in the practice of tolerance and patience.

PAD

THE FOURTH SYLLABLE "PAD"

helps us to achieve the perfection of perseverance.

ME

THE FIFTH SYLLABLE "ME"

helps us to achieve perfection in the practice of concentration.

HUM

THE SIXTH SYLLABLE "HUM"

helps us to achieve perfection in the practice of wisdom.

Kalu Rinpoche said, "What could be more meaningful than to say the mantra and accomplish the six perfections?"

Chenrezig, Buddha of compassion, is another name for Avalokiteshvara. Chenrezig and his love and compassion are within us. When we see the visual of the Buddha, we connect with the One Mind. The confusion of the speech aspect of our Being is transformed into enlightened awareness. This love and compassion is the source of empowerment of the Johrei energies that come from within us!

With regard to the history of Asia in the 5th century C.E., Avalokiteshvara was known in China as a male Being of Light and compassion. In the 2nd millennium, Avalokiteshvara was known in China as the female Being of Light "Kwan Yin" who is much like the Blessed Mother Mary. She represents loving kindness and help in time of need, bringing male children to childless mothers. She has soft energy.

To the Japanese, Avalokiteshvara is known as Kannon. There was a period of 300 years where Christianity was banned, and the statues of Maria Kannon looked very much like the Mother Mary.

To the Tibetans, Avalokiteshvara is also known as Chenrizig.

Johrei energy is a fire energy that is similar to Reiki in use, although with slight differences. The analogy is used that Reiki is like looking with a flashlight and Johrei is like turning on the light. Reiki has more of a vibratory feel to it like electricity, or like feeling the water running through a water hose. Reiki is more tightly focused. Johrei is more of a fire-energy like basking in the sun.

Johrei uses a sacred wall hanging with altar. Prayers are made to Kannon and Avalokiteshvara to assist us in bringing in the Johrei energies. Johrei energies are particularly good at chasing down negative energies and consuming them. They cleanse the spirit, restore peace, and restore balance. They are also great for healing and manifesting. The sacred calligraphy of Johrei gives off a tremendous Light when hung in a sacred place in the home or temple. The "Hikari" symbol for Light is also used in Johrei.

These great energies of compassion are part of our innate nature. We pray to Avalokiteshvara and Maria Kannon to raise our vibration and help us to become one with Buddha Mind. May the Johrei energies for humanity stream forward through us!

Note: Karen "Noor" Wyse introduced me to working with Johrei energies and Avalokiteshvara and Maria Kannon, in Denver in 1987. I have used Johrei in healing work for the past 24 years.

Clearing with Earth Energies

The energies for earth clearing are the same as the Sacred Elements that are invoked with the Sacred Medicine Wheel. Earth clearing involves the right hand facing the direction of North and the left hand facing down towards Grandmother-Mother Earth.

The energy from the direction of North involves opening the door for practical level energies to come in and release stress and sadness being held in the organs of the body. The energies that come from the North carry aspects of Earth-consciousness and practical awareness of issues that we've neglected to feel and which have yet to be released.

It involves purification and a flow that feels like an electric surge/vibration and a flow of water rushing through our physical vessel to ground.

We may call in our spirit guides that help us to learn the spiritual lessons we have chosen to learn in this lifetime. In addition, we may call in our spirit animals that help us to be empowered and to express our physical nature in balance with our higher path.

We want to move ahead with our lofty ideals but sometimes forget that we first must clear and resolve past emotions and experiences from our physical body and cellular memory. Quite often, these past experiences prevent our moving ahead until we clear our energy field and release those pent-up emotions.

This is an ongoing process that allows us to keep moving ahead with our soul's agenda. Whenever we do not spend more than half the time working on ourselves, life's frustrations tend to well up inside and overwhelm us, preventing us from going forward with our original plans.

A once or twice per day meditation to call in spirit guides, spirit animals, communicator guides, and the Sacred Elements will help us to release stress and tears from our energy fields and physical bodies. This process can be used as often as necessary.

Clearing our physical body and energy field makes an excellent complement to eating a balanced diet with much less sugar, less meat, and more vegetables and fruits. If we do eat meat, then free-range cattle, cage-free chicken, and wild fish are better choices for our health. Eating natural foods rather than processed and treated foods is becoming more important all the time. Healthy eating habits and energy clearing on a regular basis keeps us well and able to process through life's challenges. It keeps us prepared for times when life brings us stressful situations to deal with. Regular energy clearing brings clarity and keeps us free from attracting so much drama into our lives as well. Meditation brings us close to guidance and aids on our spiritual path.

The first thing to do is to remember a time in our past when we connected with Earth Energies in meditation, or an experience of connecting with Sacred Elements in a medicine wheel. We may invoke our connection to Mother Earth in grounding, or visualize a cord surging down from our spine and attaching to the center of Earth's axis. We can reconnect with the feeling of our feet heating up and our base chakra vibrating as it opens to Mother Earth.

In any case, we call forth our spirit guides, our spirit animals, communicator guides, and power animals, and we sit facing the South for release. If we are assisting someone else, then *they* sit facing the South for release and *we* sit facing the North to facilitate.

The energies here all work together for our peace and well-being. They encompass spirit guides on many levels including communicator guides and animal wisdom (owl medicine) plus the Element of Earth from the North and the blue-green color of water rushing through us. Our senses come into play as we not only *see* the blue-green of water and *hear* the rushing of water through us, but we also become aware by *listening* to our communicator guides regarding the issues that we may be feeling as discomfort in our body. We visualize the cause of discomfort in our mind's eye. We ask Mother Earth if She will take it from us as it no longer serves us.

We feel our energy field build, then *"woosh!"* We feel and see the causes of discomfort release and wash through our body. This gives us strength of clarity for self-change.

Please refer to the section called "Earth Energy Clearing and Healing" in Chapter VI for an outline and procedure for clearing.

In conclusion, we have the words of the accomplished master Osho who said, "Be practical, expect a miracle!"

Continue this amazing journey
with me in this
Bringing In the Light Series!

Visit my website at
<u>www.AngelsGrace.org</u>
to obtain more books in this series.

Prayers for All Occasions
BRINGING IN THE LIGHT SERIES
Book I

MYSTIC
BRINGING IN THE LIGHT SERIES
Book II
(Check website for details.)

IN GRATITUDE

When we choose our Higher Self as the truth of who we are, a transformation takes place. The Light takes us on a fabulous adventure!

Thank you for the opportunity to share some of my spiritual and energetic discoveries.

I leave you with these thoughts to contemplate.

Be diligent, attend to basics, expect miracles!

◆

In Gratitude, In Service to the Light,

Expanding, Extending to personal consciousness and Blessing all humankind.

Blessings of Love and Light for your journey!

Namasté

John

About the Author

Author and healer, John Pollock, is a "Bringer of Light" and energy worker, facilitating Cosmic Fire and Illumination to advance the quickening of spirit and personal transformation. His awakening and great heart connection enables him to hold a Sacred Space with Spirit for expansion and a shift in awareness!

Visit his website at www.AngelsGrace.org

www.ingramcontent.com/pod-product-compliance
Lightning Source LLC
Chambersburg PA
CBHW060019100426
42740CB00010B/1531